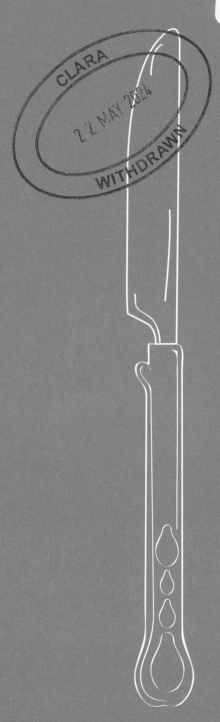

THE
IRISH COUNTRYWOMEN'S ASSOCIATION
COOKBOOK

THE
IRISH COUNTRYWOMEN'S ASSOCIATION

COOKBOOK

Recipes from our homes to yours

General Editor Aoife Carrigy

GILL & MACMILLAN

GILL & MACMILLAN
Hume Avenue, Park West, Dublin 12
with associated companies throughout the world
www.gillmacmillanbooks.ie

© IRISH COUNTRYWOMEN'S TRUST, 2012
978 07171 5332 9

General Editor Aoife Carrigy
Index compiled by Cover to Cover
Design and print origination by Tanya M Ross, Elementinc.ie
Printed by Printer Trento Srl, Italy
Photography by Joanne Murphy
Styled by Orla Neligan
Recipes tested by Marie McGuirk
Assistant to photographer and stylist: Niamh Freeney

PROPS SUPPLIED BY
Avoca: H/O, Kilmacanogue, Bray, Co Wicklow.
T: 01 286 7466; E: info@avoca.ie; W: www.avoca.ie
Eden Home & Garden: 1–4 Temple Grove, Temple Road, Blackrock, Co Dublin. T: 01 764 2004;
E: edenhomeandgarden@hotmail.com; W: www.edenhomeandgarden.ie
Meadows & Byrne: Dublin, Cork, Galway, Clare, Tipperary. T: 01 280 5444/021 434 4100;
E: info@meadowsandbyrne.com; W: www.meadowsandbyrne.com
Marks & Spencer: Unit 1–28, Dundrum Town Centre, Dublin 16. T: 01 299 1300; W: www.marksandspencer.ie
Cath Kidston: Level 1 Unit 49, Dundrum Town Centre, Dublin 16. T: 01 296 4430; E: dundrum@cathkidston.co.uk; W: cathkidston.co.uk
House of Fraser: Dundrum Town Centre, Dublin 16. T: 01 299 1400; E: dundrum@hof.co.uk; W: houseoffraser.co.uk
The Blue Door: The Crescent, Monkstown, Co Dublin.
T: 01 230 1894; E: customerservice@thebluedoordirect.ie; W: www.thebluedoordirect.ie
Historic Interiors: Oberstown, Lusk, Co Dublin. T: 01 843 7174; E: killian@historicinteriors.net
Harold's Bazaar: 208 Harold's Cross Road, Dublin 6. T: 087 722 8789.
All photographs supplied by Joanne Murphy except the following:
© Alexey Ivanov / Getty Images, p68; © Emmeline Watkins / Alamy, p108

1 3 5 4 2

Contents

MAIN MEALS

Vegetarian

Seafood

White Meat

Red Meat

ON THE SIDE

Vegetables & Salads

Dips, Sauces & Stocks

Puddings & Desserts

APPENDICES

INDEX

Introduction

Over the 100 years of the history of the Irish Countrywomen's Association, a variety of local cookbooks have been written by individual ICA Guilds and their members. The aim of the earliest books produced was to be a practical guide to help women improve their culinary skills. These early books were passed down through families from one generation to the next. I am lucky enough to have a very well-used and well-loved ICA cookery book, *Bantracht na Tuaitha: 1910–1960 Golden Jubilee Cookery Book*, as part of my family's heritage. When I came into office as National President of the ICA, we felt the time had come to ask my fellow members to join me in contributing some of the wonderful recipes that we use every day in our homes to make up a national cookery book of the ICA's favourite dishes.

We wanted to include dishes featuring produce local to our area and recipes enjoyed in a family for generations alongside modern ideas picked up along the way, and in doing so to build up a new collection of recipes that span the length and breadth of the country. And we wanted to pepper these with practical tips for saving time and money, for getting the best results every time and for cooking for special diets in order to share the wealth of our members' experience and to preserve this knowledge for future generations.

We in the ICA are very proud of our heritage and of all the milestones that we have collectively achieved over the last 100 years. This cookery book is not only a celebration of the wonderful ingredients and produce available in this great land, but also of our colourful history, our families, our local communities.

When the ICA was established in 1910, its aim was to improve the standard of life in rural Ireland through education and co-operative effort. Since its beginnings the ICA has been part of all of the key developmental activities in food and its production in Ireland. Up until the late 1920s, potatoes, cabbages and onions were the only vegetables grown and cooked throughout Ireland. The ICA bought and distributed a wide variety of seeds, and taught members how to grow and cook these new vegetables at what was the first ICA summer school, held in Sliabh na mBán, Co Tipperary in 1929.

In the 1930s these ICA classes expanded to cover poultry and egg production, cheese-making and bee-keeping to enable members improve their diets and earn money from the sale of their home produce. In response to Ireland's tuberculosis epidemic in the earlier part of the last century the ICA encouraged members to keep goats whose milk was free from TB infection, and goats' milk depots were set up around the country to enable members to trade.

By 1947 the ICA was involved in helping small producers to collectively market their home produce by setting up a nationwide network of Country Markets. In the 1950s the rural electrification of Ireland transformed the kitchens of Irish women and their families. Members of the ICA toured the country with a Model Farm Kitchen mobile unit, demonstrating the greatly improved cooking facilities now available. In the 1960s the ICA's 'Turn on the Tap' group water scheme gave rural families the basic necessity of running water inside the home, improving hygiene and cooking as a result.

Now in the 21st Century, food and the joys of cooking continue to be an integral part of ICA life. We continue to offer cookery and gardening classes at An Grianán, our adult education centre in Termonfeckin, Co Louth where RTE's ICA *Bootcamp* was filmed. In 2011 we joined forces with TV chef and food writer Edward Hayden, who embarked on a county-by-county road show of cookery demonstrations, an initiative that has proved extremely popular with members right across the country.

In today's busy modern lives, the importance of a family meal cannot be overstated. It is around the family table that we learn so much about our values, where we right the wrongs of the day and discuss our problems and hopes for the future. The family meal is central to our communities and their wellbeing. *The ICA Cookbook* will help you make this experience the best it can be, and help us all rediscover the simple pleasures of a home-cooked meal made with local produce that is in season and good for our health.

As we have sung in our ICA song for the last 100 years, our land "is a rich and rare land, she is a fresh and fair land". Let us enjoy what is all around us, both rich and fresh, and let us celebrate our heritage through the simple pleasures of home-cooked food.

Liz Wall
National President of the Irish Countrywomen's Association

Contained in the following pages is a unique collection of recipes focused on tried and tested dishes from the homes of ordinary women from all over the country. Some of these women prefer to cook their food from scratch every time, down to using home-made stocks, sauces and pastries. Others believe life is too short to boil bones or roll your own puff pastry; these women have fridges, freezers and larders well-stocked with reliable fall-back ingredients and have no problem reaching for a bottle or opening a packet to save time. Some would consider these shortcuts to be cheating, others see them as pragmatic routes to delicious dishes. Some wouldn't dream of using a microwave; others cook their fish, vegetables and even their cakes in them. The women of the ICA have never been shy of holding their own opinions, and these recipes give voice to a broad range of culinary schools of thought.

We are bombarded today with ideals of the perfect home-maker but the reality is that often we want to know how to cheat without compromising on flavour. There are other times when we want to dedicate the time to developing a new skill, so that our fridges, freezers and larders can become well-stocked with our own home-made fall-backs. This cookbook aims to satisfy both of those demands, and much else in-between.

We have also included dishes from Marie McGuirk and Edward Hayden, two of the chefs who work with the ICA on a regular basis and who pass on their culinary knowledge as tutors at An Grianán adult education centre. But for the most part these are real recipes from real women, some of whom may have trained in home economics, some of whom were trained by their grannies (many of them ICA members too), many of whom learnt from experience by cooking for their younger siblings or their growing families.

As you might expect there are lots of very traditional recipes tucked throughout these pages, many with interesting twists that take into account the changes in how we eat. Irish stew no longer needs to be cooked for hours before it is palatable, as tender lamb is available year round. Deep freezers mean bread and butter pudding is now less of a necessary frugality for using up stale bread, and more of a beloved classic – and a steady supply of fresh fruit means we can now play around with what we put into it. Indeed, in some cases we have included two different approaches to the one idea just to illustrate that there are many ways to scratch an itch.

But while many of these recipes are distinctly Irish, there are international influences too. Some of the authors of these recipes moved to Ireland from other countries, bringing with them their most treasured recipes. Others have taken a flavour of their favourite travels home to incorporate into their everyday repertoire.

Just as the women who these recipes represent are an eclectic bunch with diverse taste in home-cooked flavours, so too will the readers differ in their own culinary leanings and expertise.

Experienced cooks looking for new ideas will find much to inspire and intrigue, whether they favour shortcuts or cooking from scratch. But this cookbook will also prove an invaluable resource for the next generation of home-makers, the novice cooks still building up confidence in the kitchen who might call home for that foolproof recipe – or might reach for this book instead. Think of *The ICA Cookbook* as akin to having not just your own mammy on speed dial but rather a whole host of mammies and grannies from all over the country, each sharing their own words of wisdom and precious firsthand experiences.

A WORD FROM THE GUEST CHEFS

Marie McGuirk, resident chef and cookery tutor at An Grianán

My mother's tried and tested recipes and a lot of trial and error with new recipes; an apron, a wooden spoon and a well-stocked larder; a humming stove and a bustling family home: all of these things have moulded me into who I am today. I grew up on a farm where the front door was always open, the kettle was always on the boil and there was always something fresh coming out of the oven. Growing up reliant on the land and with an awareness of the seasons gave me an appreciation for eating foods that are local and where possible in season in order to get the best from ingredients.

Over thirty years ago I became involved with the ICA and An Grianán adult education centre. From the start, I embraced the ethos of this wonderful college which was entrusted to the ICA for the health, education and welfare of the people of Ireland. As a cookery tutor, my aim has been to empower people to cook simple ingredients well and produce wonderful meals with as little effort as possible. I am very passionate about buying local produce and utilising all the best resources from local suppliers and this very much reflects the philosophy of the ICA.

As a food writer for magazines and newspapers, I am also aware of the challenges faced by today's world in which the art of home cooking and various domestic skills has skipped a generation. I hope that in some way this cookery book can help to address this gap, and inspire a new generation.

Marie McGuirk

The ICA is very grateful to Marie for sharing with us some of her favourite recipes from her own home and from the kitchen of An Grianán.

Edward Hayden, TV chef and food writer

Cooking is such a joy for so many people, giving them an opportunity to relax whilst both preparing the meal and entertaining family and friends. What better way to share that joy than through a cookery book, and particularly one that represents the kitchens of so many homes around Ireland?

It is my privilege to have been asked by ICA National President Liz Wall and her team to contribute some recipes to this cookery book and to be involved with the wonderfully dynamic and innovative group that is the Irish Countrywomen's Association. Long before I got involved in my current capacity, my family enjoyed a great familiarity with and respect for the ICA. My first cousin Maureen Holden spent over 20 years working with the organisation at national level. I remember with great fondness a trip I took to Lake Garda with Maureen and some former national presidents, officers and friends of the ICA. The happenings of that holiday would make for a great book in itself!

Now a number of years later I have just completed a national cookery roadshow with the ICA and Kinane Kitchens, in which we did a series of cookery evenings and demonstrations for each ICA County Federation. It was great to travel around the country and meet the grassroots members who continue to practise those core values that are quintessential to the ICA. In recent times I have also joined the team of tutors at the wonderful An Grianán adult education centre to teach and demonstrate the art of cookery. Each time I visit, the range and diversity of courses offered amazes me, as does the level of commitment and dedication that is employed at An Grianán.

Food styles and trends have evolved in recent years, but the art of home entertaining has never waned in popularity. There is something very satisfying about spending time preparing and serving a delicious home-cooked meal to your family and friends. I have no doubt but that this book will be of great benefit as you carry on what has been one of the most essential acts since time began – that of cooking.

With every good wish to the officers and members of the Irish Countrywomen's Association in their continued work for the organisation.
Happy cooking!

Edward Hayden
The ICA is very grateful to Edward for sharing
some of his favourite recipes with us in this book.

Chapter 1
To Start

Soups, Salads & Starters

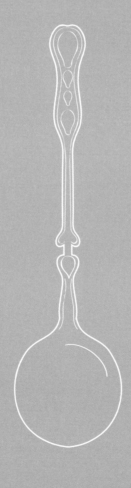

Carrot Soup

AUDREY STARRETT, DONEGAL: JACK OF ALL TRADES

This recipe came about because a member of my family is a vegetarian but it soon became a favourite amongst us all. The sweetness of the carrots makes it extremely popular with children.

Serves 4–6
- 25g (1oz) butter
- 1 medium onion, chopped
- 1 bay leaf
- 4–5 medium carrots, scraped and diced
- 1 small potato, peeled and diced
- 400ml (¾ pint) water
- 400ml (¾ pint) milk
- salt and freshly ground black pepper

to garnish
- 1 handful chopped fresh chives
- fresh cream (optional)

1. In a large heavy-based saucepan over a gentle heat, sweat the onion and bay leaf in a little melted butter for about five minutes, or until soft and translucent. Add the carrot and potato and fry gently for a further seven minutes.

2. Pour in water, cover and bring to the boil. Simmer gently for about 20 minutes or until vegetables are cooked.

3. Allow to cool a little, remove the bay leaf and liquidise in a blender. Pour back into the saucepan, add milk and heat through gently. Season to taste and serve garnished with chopped chives and maybe a swirl of fresh cream for an extra treat.

Asparagus Soup

MARIE MCGUIRK, LOUTH: COOKERY TUTOR AND ASPIRING GOLFER

This soup is best made in late spring or early summer when local asparagus is in season, and makes an elegant soup with which to start a special dinner.

Serves 4

- 2 tablespoons olive oil
- 2 onions, finely chopped
- 250g (9oz) asparagus, finely chopped
- 500ml (1 pint) chicken or vegetable stock, hot (see p111 for recipe)
- salt and freshly ground black pepper
- 4 tablespoons double cream

1. Heat the olive oil in a large saucepan over a gentle heat. Add the onion and sweat for four minutes until soft and translucent. Add the asparagus and cook for another two minutes.

2. Add the stock and bring to the boil. Season to taste and reduce the heat to simmer for about five minutes, or until the asparagus is cooked through.

3. Add the cream and blitz with a hand blender until smooth.

Spring Nettle Soup

ANNETTE DUNNE, CAVAN: WORKING GRANDMOTHER WHO LOVES READING

My mother used to make this for us as a springtime tonic, being full of iron and other nutrients. As well as being really good for you it's very tasty, especially if you pick tender young leaves. Do wear gloves when handling the nettles, and harvest away from the roadside.

Serves 8
- 225g (8oz) young nettle leaves
- 50g (2oz) butter
- 350g (12oz) potatoes, peeled and chopped
- 175g (6oz) onions, chopped
- 175g (6oz) leeks, chopped
- salt and freshly ground black pepper
- 1 litre (2 pints) chicken stock (see p111 for recipe)
- 150ml (¼ pint) cream, plus a little extra to garnish

ICA Tip

A piece of parchment or even an old butter wrapper placed over sweating vegetables helps to keep the moisture in while cooking gently.

1. Soak nettles prior to cooking to draw out sting and rinse well.

2. Melt the butter in a heavy-based saucepan over a medium heat. When it foams add potatoes, onions and leeks and toss them until well coated. Season, cover with piece of parchment (see Tip) and then with the saucepan lid, and sweat gently over a low heat for 12–15 minutes or until the vegetables are soft but not browned.

3. Remove paper lid, add stock and gently boil for about 10 minutes or until vegetables are cooked. Add the chopped nettles and simmer uncovered for about five minutes, taking care not to overcook or the vegetables will lose their flavour.

4. Add the cream, remove from the heat and allow to cool a little before liquidising. Check seasoning and serve garnished with a swirl of cream.

Chilled Avocado Soup

LIZ WALL, WICKLOW: BUSY MUM AND ICA NATIONAL PRESIDENT

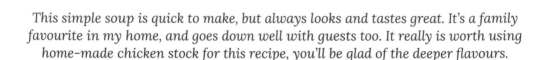

This simple soup is quick to make, but always looks and tastes great. It's a family favourite in my home, and goes down well with guests too. It really is worth using home-made chicken stock for this recipe, you'll be glad of the deeper flavours.

Serves 4–6
- 2 avocados
- 500ml (1 pint) cold chicken stock (see p111 for recipe)
- 125ml (4fl oz) sour cream
- 125ml (4fl oz) cream
- 1 small onion, finely chopped
- 2 tablespoons lemon juice
- ½ teaspoon salt

to garnish
- 4 handfuls fresh coriander leaves, chopped

1. Scoop out the avocado flesh and purée with the stock, creams and onion. You may need to add more stock or water if the soup is too thick as consistency will vary according to the size of avocado used.

2. Season to taste with the lemon juice and salt, and chill for at least an hour.

3. Serve garnished with chopped coriander.

Cream of Mushroom Soup

NUALA COSTELLO, LAOIS: MOTHER OF FOUR WHO LOVES TO COOK AND BAKE

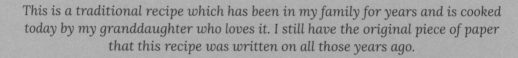

This is a traditional recipe which has been in my family for years and is cooked today by my granddaughter who loves it. I still have the original piece of paper that this recipe was written on all those years ago.

Serves 8

- 175g (6oz) butter
- 350g (12oz) onions, finely chopped
- 450g (1lb) button mushrooms, wiped and chopped
- 50g (2oz) flour
- 1½ litres (3 pints) chicken stock (see p111 for recipe)
- 275ml (½ pint) milk
- 1 teaspoon ground black pepper
- 1 teaspoon sugar
- 1 lemon, juice only (to taste)

to serve

- 2 handfuls croutons (optional)
- home-made brown bread

1. Melt the butter in a large heavy-based saucepan. Gently sweat the onions for 10 minutes until softened but not browned.

2. Add mushrooms, cover and continue to cook for a further 10 minutes. Stir in flour and cook for three minutes.

3. Slowly add stock, stirring continuously. Bring to the boil and simmer slowly for 20 minutes. Stir in the milk, season with salt and pepper and then with the lemon juice to taste.

4. Simmer gently for a further 10 minutes but do not allow to boil after adding the milk.

5. Serve hot, garnished with croutons.

Quick Vegetable Soup

LIZ WALL, WICKLOW: BUSY MUM AND ICA NATIONAL PRESIDENT

This quick, tasty snack has been cooked for years in my family, and remains a great family favourite across all generations. We still enjoy it on a weekly basis.

Serves 4
- 2 medium onions, peeled
- 2–3 garlic cloves, peeled
- 1 head of celery, trimmed
- 1 red pepper, cored
- 1 green pepper, cored
- 1 stock cube
- salt and freshly ground black pepper

ICA *Tip*
A quick soup like this captures the flavour, colour and nutrients of the vegetables, so take care not to boil for longer than necessary.

1. Roughly chop all the vegetables and place in a large saucepan. Just cover with water, crumble in the stock cube and bring to the boil.

2. Cook at a rolling boil for ten minutes, reduce the heat and leave simmering until soft enough to purée. Season to taste.

Fresh Tomato & Bean Soup

MARGARET O'REILLY, CORK: PRIZE-WINNING MAKER OF CARRICKMACROSS LACE

I found this recipe in a cookbook I picked up in a charity shop and over the years I've added a bit of this and that. Although it's a great way to showcase fresh tomatoes in season, you can also use tinned tomatoes making this a versatile all-weather soup.

Serves 4–6

- 900g (2lb) ripe plum tomatoes
- 2 tablespoons olive oil
- 2 medium onions, roughly chopped
- 3 garlic cloves, crushed
- 1 litre (2 pints) vegetable stock
- 2 tablespoons sun-dried tomato paste
- 2 teaspoons paprika
- salt and freshly ground black pepper
- 1 tablespoon cornflour
- 400g (14oz) cooked cannellini beans, rinsed and drained
- 400g (14oz) cooked kidney beans, rinsed and drained
- 2 tablespoons chopped fresh coriander

to serve
- fresh ciabatta or brown bread

1. First, peel the tomatoes. Using a sharp knife, make a small cross in each one and place in a bowl. Pour over boiling water to cover and leave to stand for a minute before draining. The skins should peel off easily. Quarter them and then cut each piece in half again.

2. Heat the oil in a large heavy-based saucepan and sweat the onions and garlic for a few minutes, until softened. Add the tomatoes together with the stock, sun-dried tomato paste and paprika. Season, bring to the boil and simmer for 10 minutes.

3. Mix the cornflour to a paste with a couple of tablespoons of water and stir this into the soup along with the beans. Cook for a further five minutes, check seasoning and adjust if necessary. Stir in the chopped coriander just before serving, and serve with ciabatta or brown bread.

ICA Tip
If you don't have sun-dried tomato paste you could substitute with some sun-dried tomato pesto.

Cauliflower & Bacon Soup with Cheese Toasties

MARIE MCGUIRK, LOUTH: COOKERY TUTOR AND ASPIRING GOLFER

This soup is perfect comfort food and, served together with the moreish cheese toasties, makes a fairly substantial lunch. Leave out the toasties if you'd like to serve it as a starter, or try making a couple of them and cutting into cheesey croutons.

Serves 4–6

- 2 tablespoons vegetable oil
- 1 large or 2 small onions, chopped
- 8 streaky bacon rashers
- 2 potatoes, chopped
- 1 small cauliflower, cut into florets and leaves sliced
- 500ml (1 pint) vegetable stock
- 250ml (½ pint) milk
- salt and freshly ground black pepper

for the cheese toasties (optional)

- 8 slices French bread
- 4 teaspoons Dijon mustard
- 110g (4oz) cheddar, grated

1. Heat the oil in a large heavy-based saucepan, and sweat the onion for five minutes or until softened. Chop two rashers, add to the pan and fry for a further two minutes. Stir in the potatoes and cauliflower and mix well. Add the stock and bring to the boil. Cover and simmer for 15 minutes until the vegetables are tender. Meanwhile, preheat the grill to medium.

2. Allow soup to cool a little before blitzing in a blender or food processor (you'll have to do this in two batches). Return to the pan and stir in the milk. Reheat gently and season to taste.

3. Meanwhile, grill the remaining bacon until crisp, drain on kitchen paper and chop into pieces. If serving the cheese toasties, toast the bread slices on one side, spread mustard over the untoasted sides and sprinkle with the grated cheese. Grill until the cheese is melted and golden.

4. Serve the soup sprinkled with the grilled bacon pieces and with the cheese toasties on the side.

Butternut Squash Soup

MARIE MCGUIRK, LOUTH: COOKERY TUTOR AND ASPIRING GOLFER

Butternut squash store very well making this soup a great autumnal fall-back recipe. Its warm flavours are nicely cheerful when the days are starting to draw in. You could substitute with pumpkin, which can be a handy way to use up scooped-out pumpkin flesh at Halloween.

Serves 4–6
- 1kg (2lb) butternut squash or pumpkin, unpeeled
- 1 tablespoon sunflower oil
- salt and freshly ground black pepper
- 25g (1oz) butter
- 1 medium onion, chopped
- 4 sprigs fresh thyme, leaves picked
- 1 litre (2 pints) vegetable stock, hot
- 150ml (¼ pint) single cream
- 50g (2oz) Gruyère cheese, coarsely grated

ICA Tip
  Squash have thick skins, making them hard to peel while raw. Use a sharp knife and place a wet cloth under the chopping board to prevent slipping.

1. Preheat oven to 200°C/400°F/Gas 6. With a sharp knife, chop the squash into chunky wedges. Rub with oil, season well and place into one large or two smaller roasting tins, skin-side down. Roast in preheated oven for 30 minutes, or until tender. Remove from the oven and set aside to cool a little.

2. Meanwhile melt the butter in a large heavy-based saucepan. Add the onion and half the thyme leaves, cover and gently sweat for about 10 minutes or until the onion is very soft but not browned.

3. When the roasted squash is cool enough to handle, slice away and discard the skin and chop the remaining flesh into small chunks. Add these to the softened onion along with the stock and a teaspoon of salt. Cover and simmer gently for 10 minutes.

4. Allow the soup to cool slightly, add most of the remaining thyme leaves and blitz in a blender until smooth. Return to a clean pan and bring back to a gentle simmer. Stir in the cream and season to taste.

5. Serve with a little of the grated Gruyère in each bowl and scatter over the remaining thyme leaves.

Chicken & Pecan Salad

STEPHANIE IGOE, LONGFORD: VOLUNTEER AND BUSY MUM OF THREE

This is a favourite family recipe and because we have such an extended family we make it quite regularly. The contrast between the grapes and pecans makes it a very popular dish. The quantities can be easily increased for larger numbers, it can be made in advance and keeps well.

Serves 4
- 3 cooked chicken breasts
- 450g (1lb) seedless green grapes, halved
- 4 generous handfuls pecan halves
- 4 celery sticks, diced
- ½ bunch fresh dill, finely chopped
- 375ml (12fl oz) sour cream or yoghurt
- 375ml (12fl oz) mayonnaise
- salt and freshly ground black pepper

to serve
- 4 handfuls watercress or other greens
- 1 handful fresh dill sprigs

1. Shred cooked chicken into bite-sized pieces and place in mixing bowl with grapes, pecans, celery and chopped dill.

2. In a separate bowl mix sour cream and mayonnaise, add to chicken mixture and season. Stir to coat well, cover and refrigerate for two hours.

3. Serve on bed of watercress or other fresh greens and garnish with dill sprigs.

Pan-fried Prawns with Lemon & Garlic

MARIE O'TOOLE, DUBLIN: PASSIONATE GARDENER AND ASPIRING WRITER

This tasty summer dish is a version of a recipe that my grandmother used for years and it remains a favourite of mine. I live close to Howth in north County Dublin, which has superb supplies of Dublin Bay prawns.

Serves 4
- 2 tablespoons olive oil
- 2 garlic cloves, crushed
- 12–16 fresh prawns, shell on or off
- 1 large lemon, zest and juice
- pinch of paprika (optional)

to serve
- salad leaves
- brown bread

ICA *Tip*
You could use frozen prawns but it really is worth seeking out Irish prawns (also known as langoustine) as an alternative to imported ones such as tiger prawns.

1. Gently heat olive oil in a large pan over a low heat. Add garlic and cook gently for about 30 seconds, taking care not to burn.

2. Add prawns, increase the heat and cook briskly for two to three minutes, depending on size. Add the lemon zest and finish with lemon juice to taste.

3. Arrange prawns on serving plates and drizzle with the cooking juices. Serve with salad leaves and brown bread for mopping, and don't forget to provide guests with napkins and a finger bowl, especially if serving with shells on. This is a dish that demands sticky fingers!

Grilled Peach with Herbed Cheese

BRID MALONE, LAOIS: MOTHER OF FIVE, WALKER AND SWIMMER

The sweet and savoury flavours make a great contrast in this attractive starter. The pâté itself can be served on toast as a snack or as part of a spread for a party.

Serves 4–6
- 1 tin yellow peaches, halved

for the herbed cheese pâté
- 140g (5oz) butter
- 450g (1lb) cream cheese
- 3 garlic cloves, crushed with a little salt
- 1 tablespoon finely chopped fresh chervil
- 1 tablespoon finely chopped fresh parsley
- 1 tablespoon finely chopped fresh chives

for the garnish
- 1 orange, peel or zest only
- 2 handfuls watercress
- 1 handful croutons (optional)

ICA Tip
Try poaching fresh peaches as per the poached pear recipe (see p22) and using in place of the tinned peaches.

1. To make the pâté, melt butter slowly in saucepan and allow to cool. Combine the cheese, garlic and herbs in a large mixing bowl, mixing well to ensure the herbs are evenly distributed. When the melted butter has cooled pour into the cream cheese mixture, folding gently to mix. Transfer to a loaf tin and chill to set or until ready to use.

2. When ready to serve, preheat oven to 180°C/350°F/Gas 4 and preheat a grill to hot. Place a dollop of herbed cheese pâté into the centre of each peach half. Warm through in preheated oven for about 15 minutes and finish off under the grill.

3. Garnish with a twist of orange or sprinkling of zest, a sprig or two of watercress and maybe a scattering of croutons.

Roast Red Peppers with Basil Pesto

MARIE MCGUIRK, LOUTH: COOKERY TUTOR AND ASPIRING GOLFER

This is a versatile dish that works great with any kind of soft cheese, from goats' cheese to Camembert-style to a herbed cream cheese. It makes a really quick but elegant starter – or you could also increase the quantity of the filling and serve as a main course.

Serves 4
- 2 red peppers
- 1 handful basil leaves
- 8 semi-dried tomatoes
- 4–8 baby cherry tomatoes, halved
- 100g (3½oz) soft cheese
- 3–4 tablespoons basil pesto (see p106)
- 2 tablespoons olive oil
- salt and freshly ground black pepper

to serve
- 3–4 tablespoons olive oil
- 1 tablespoon balsamic vinegar
- 4 generous handfuls salad leaves

1. Preheat oven to 180°C/350°F/Gas 4.

2. Cut peppers in half, remove seeds and place in an ovenproof baking dish. Into each pepper half, layer a basil leaf and a couple each of semi-dried tomatoes and cherry tomatoes. Add a tablespoon of soft cheese to each and top with a couple of teaspoons of pesto.

3. Season, drizzle over a little oil and cover the dish loosely with foil. Roast in preheated oven for about 30 minutes, removing foil halfway through the cooking.

4. Shake the olive oil and balsamic vinegar in a jam jar to emulsify. Serve the roast peppers while hot with salad leaves drizzled with balsamic dressing.

Blue Cheese, Pear & Walnut Salad

BREDA MCDONALD, KILKENNY: PASSIONATE BELIEVER IN LOCAL COMMUNITY

*I love blue cheese and the diverse flavour combinations in this salad work
exceptionally well, giving sweet, salty, nutty and peppery flavours in every
mouthful. And because of the variation in colour, as well as being super healthy,
this dish is also visually impressive.*

Serves 4
- 4 large firm pears
- 110g (4oz) sugar
- 1 lemon, cut into wedges
- 1 orange, cut into wedges
- 1 glass of white wine
- 225g (8oz) blue cheese, cut into chunks or crumbled
- 16–20 walnuts, halved
- 1 large handful fresh rocket

to garnish
- freshly ground black pepper
- sprigs of fresh parsley or chervil

1. Carefully peel the pears trying in so far as possible to retain their shape. In a large pot combine the sugar, lemon and orange wedges and white wine with a pint of water. Immerse the pears in the sweetened liquids.

2. Bring the mixture slowly to the boil and simmer for 20–30 minutes, adding extra water if required to keep the pears fully immersed. Test the pears with a cocktail stick: when softened remove the pot from the heat and set aside to cool in the liquor.

3. Once cool, remove pears from liquid and core with a sharp knife, cutting from the base. Keeping the pear whole, slice three-quarters of the way from the core up towards the top. You are aiming to fan the sliced pear while keeping the stem-end intact. If this is proving tricky, you can simply slice each pear.

4. Pile the rocket into the centre of a serving plate or divide between four individual plates. Fan or slice the poached pears on top of the rocket. Scatter around blue cheese and walnuts and drizzle with a little of the poaching liquor. To finish, you could crack some black pepper across the top of the pears and garnish with a sprig of fresh parsley or chervil.

Pan-Fried Smoked Salmon & Couscous Salad

MARGARET O'REILLY, CORK: PRIZE-WINNING MAKER OF CARRICKMACROSS LACE

This recipe was a winner in the 2010 ICA Gempack Recipe Competition. I like to let people help themselves to the yoghurt dip and couscous salad, making it a convivial way to start a meal. It also makes for a nice lunchtime main course.

Serves 8–10 as a starter

- 450g (1lb) smoked salmon, sliced
- 2 tablespoons pinenuts, toasted
- ½ lemon, grated rind only
- 2–3 handfuls crisp lettuce leaves

for the yoghurt dip

- 250g (9oz) Greek-style yoghurt
- 85g (3oz) cucumber, finely chopped
- 1 tablespoon lemon juice

for the couscous

- 3 tablespoons olive oil
- 5 spring onions, chopped
- 1 garlic clove, crushed
- 1 teaspoon ground cumin
- 350ml (12fl oz) vegetable stock
- 175g (6oz) couscous
- 2 tomatoes, peeled (see Tip) and chopped
- 4 tablespoons chopped fresh parsley
- 4 tablespoons chopped fresh mint
- 1 fresh green chilli, deseeded and finely chopped
- 2 tablespoons lemon juice
- salt and freshly ground black pepper

1. To make the couscous, heat the oil in a heavy-based saucepan, add the spring onions and garlic and cook over a gentle heat for about 60 seconds. Stir in the cumin and cook for another minute or until it begins to release its aromas.

2. Add the stock and increase the heat to bring to the boil. Remove from the heat, stir in the couscous, cover and leave to stand for 10 minutes, until the couscous has swelled and all the liquid has been absorbed.

3. Transfer to a large mixing bowl and stir in the tomatoes, parsley, mint, chilli and lemon juice. Season to taste and leave to stand for up to an hour to allow flavours to develop. When ready to serve, line a bowl with crisp lettuce leaves and spoon the couscous salad into the centre. Scatter over the toasted pinenuts and grated lemon rind to garnish.

4. For the yoghurt dip, mix together the Greek-style yoghurt, cucumber and lemon juice, and transfer to a small serving bowl.

5. Heat a non-stick frying pan, add the smoked salmon and cook for just a few seconds on each side on the dry pan. Divide the salmon between individual serving plates and serve immediately, allowing people to help themselves to couscous and dip.

ICA Tip

To peel tomatoes, simply cut a cross in the top, cover them with boiling water for a minute or two and drain. The skin should peel away easily.

Quick Spiced Beef with Orange Cream

MAIREAD O'CARROLL, CORK: MOTHER OF SIX WHO LOVES ENTERTAINING

I fell in love with spiced beef when I moved to Cork, where it takes pride of place at every butcher's counter at Christmas. This recipe allows me have my own supply all year round. It's delicious as a cold starter or hot main course with mashed potatoes and green vegetables.

Serves 6–8

- 2kg (4lb) corned beef, silverside or tailend
- 3 tablespoons dark brown sugar
- 1 tablespoon coarsely ground black pepper
- 1 tablespoon coriander seeds, crushed
- 1 tablespoon juniper berries, crushed
- 3 teaspoons allspice
- 2 teaspoons ground ginger
- 1 teaspoon ground cloves
- 2 bay leaves, crushed
- 1 small onion, finely chopped
- 250ml (½ pint) Guinness

to serve (optional)

- 200g (7oz) sour cream or crème fraîche
- 1–2 tablespoons chopped chives
- 1–2 garlic cloves, grated
- 1–2 tablespoons finely grated orange rind
- freshly ground black pepper

1. To spice the beef, mix together the sugar, spices, herbs and onion and rub into the meat. Refrigerate for three to four days, turning and rubbing daily.

2. In a large saucepan, barely cover the marinated meat with cold water. Cover with a tight lid and bring to the boil. Reduce heat and cook very gently for about 3½ hours, adding the Guinness to the cooking liquid for the last hour. When the joint is cooked remove from the heat and allow to cool in the cooking liquid before wrapping in foil and refrigerating until ready to serve (or for up to one week).

3. To serve as a starter, slice the spiced beef very thinly and serve with a little sour cream flavoured with chives, garlic, finely grated orange rind and freshly ground black pepper.

ICA Tip

Cold spiced beef is great in sandwiches with a horseradish mayonnaise or as part of a selection of cold meats for summer picnics.

HOW TO COOK FOR A CROWD

1. Keep things simple and don't fuss too much when preparing the food. Better to relax and enjoy it than to get fussed and ruin both the experience and the results.

2. Watch cookery programmes and browse cookbooks in your local library for ideas. Cook what appeals to you, and enjoy the process.

3. Don't be over-ambitious. Don't try something new when entertaining, but rather keep the experimentations for immediate family instead. If cooking something for the first time, start with simple recipes and stick to the recipe. You can always make your own modifications the next time you cook them.

4. Some dishes improve with time, particularly one-pot stews, casseroles and curries. This means you can do most of the cooking the day before and simply reheat to serve. Consider cooking dishes that can be easily reheated, or can at least be par-cooked and finished on the day.

5. Write down a task list and consider how long you need to give yourself for each task. Do as much preparation in advance as possible, and don't forget to leave time to make yourself beautiful!

6. Set the table early, or better still get someone else to do it. Recruit help where possible but delegate wisely. If you want people to help themselves to drinks, make sure they have everything they need to hand including ice and lemon.

7. Consider carefully how much food you'll need and try to have a clear idea of how many numbers you are catering for. Ask people to RSVP so that you can cater accordingly.

8. Don't overestimate quantities, especially if you plan to serve several dishes such as at a buffet-style party. Factor in the time of day you'll be eating, whether people will have eaten earlier or will plan to eat later. Remember a drinks party will need less food than an all-day family get-together.

9. Don't underestimate the quantities of food needed either. If you want to make extra food for fallback, do so with dishes that will keep well in case they don't get eaten. Dressed salads perish quickly; cold meats, cheeses and tarts keep well.

10. Remember the tips you have learnt from your mother and other family members, and pick up some of your own along the way. It's the little things that make all the difference.

Chapter 2
Main Meals

Vegetarian, Seafood,
White Meat, Red Meat

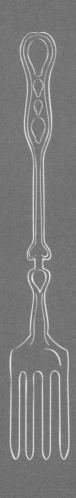

Broccoli, Cherry Tomato & Cheese Tart

MARIE MCGUIRK, LOUTH: COOKERY TUTOR AND ASPIRING GOLFER

This colourful dish will cheer up a picnic or lunchbox, eaten cold, or works well served warm with salad and potatoes for a summer's supper. You can use whatever cheese you like, from a crumbly farmhouse cheddar to soft goats' or piquant blue cheeses.

Serves 6
- 25g (1oz) butter
- 25g (1oz) plain flour
- 250ml (½ pint) milk
- 2 teaspoons wholegrain mustard
- 200g (7oz) broccoli, cut into small florets
- 200g (7oz) cherry tomatoes, quartered
- 175g (6oz) strong cheese, crumbled
- 3 eggs
- salt and freshly ground black pepper

for the pastry
- 140g (5oz) butter
- 200g (7oz) flour

to serve
- green salad
- steamed or baked potatoes

You will need
- 1 deep 25cm (10in) flan dish

ICA Tip
  Blanching vegetables is a technique used to keep the colour bright by arresting the cooking.

1. Preheat oven to 190°C/375°F/Gas 5. Grease flan dish.

2. To make the pastry, combine the flour and butter in a food processor and work the mixture until it resembles fine crumbs. Sprinkle in two to three tablespoons of cold water and pulse until the dough just clings together in a rough ball. (See p137 for tips on making pastry.)

3. Turn the dough onto a lightly floured work surface. Knead it briefly to smooth out any cracks, then roll until you have a 30cm (12in) round. Fill the greased flan dish, pressing into the corners, and trim off any excess pastry.

4. Meanwhile to make the filling, put the butter, flour and milk into a small pan. Bring slowly to the boil, whisking occasionally. Remove from heat, stir in the mustard and set aside.

5. Blanch the broccoli by cooking in boiling salted water for three minutes, draining and cooling quickly under cold running water. Drain well, then pat dry. Spread the broccoli, tomatoes and two thirds of the cheese over the pastry case.

6. Beat the eggs, stir into the mustard sauce and season well. Pour the sauce into the case, sprinkle over the remaining cheese. Bake in preheated oven for 35–40 minutes. Serve hot or cold with salad and steamed or baked potatoes.

Spinach Pie

MARY FITZGERALD, WEXFORD: GARDENER AND INTERNET ENTHUSIAST

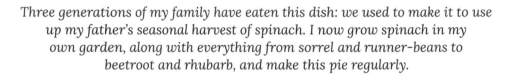

Three generations of my family have eaten this dish: we used to make it to use up my father's seasonal harvest of spinach. I now grow spinach in my own garden, along with everything from sorrel and runner-beans to beetroot and rhubarb, and make this pie regularly.

Serves 4–6
- 560g (1lb 4oz) spinach, washed
- 1 onion, chopped
- 2 eggs, beaten
- 250g (10oz) cottage cheese
- 250g (10oz) Parmesan cheese, freshly grated
- ¼ teaspoon freshly ground black pepper
- ¼ teaspoon freshly grated nutmeg

You will need
- 23cm (9in) pie dish or several smaller individual pie dishes

ICA Tip
You could cheat with a large packet of frozen spinach if you don't have any fresh spinach to hand. Simply chop and mix with the rest of the ingredients.

1. Preheat oven to 180°C/350°F/Gas 4.

2. Steam the spinach, drain well and roughly chop. In a large bowl, mix the cooked spinach with the onion, beaten eggs and both types of cheese. Beat well and season with pepper and nutmeg.

3. Transfer mixture to one large pie dish, or individual dishes if using. Bake in preheated oven for 25–30 minutes.

Courgette & Feta Frittata

AN GRIANÁN, LOUTH: ICA ADULT EDUCATION CENTRE

Once you master the basic technique behind cooking a frittata you can add whatever ingredients you like, from leftover roast chicken or cooked salmon to chorizo or roast vegetables. In this particular recipe, goats' cheese makes a nice alternative to the feta. It is worth using organic eggs, or at least free-range if possible.

Serves 4

- 6 eggs (free range or organic, if possible)
- 2 tablespoons cream or milk
- salt and freshly ground black pepper
- 1 tablespoon oil
- 1 small onion, diced finely
- 1 medium courgette, sliced thinly
- 100g (4oz) feta cheese, chopped roughly
- 1 small handful mint leaves, chopped

ICA Tip
It is worth investing in an ovenproof frying pan with a handle that can endure the heat of the oven or grill.

1. Preheat the grill to hot. In a medium-sized bowl, beat the eggs with the cream and season to taste.

2. Heat the oil in a non-stick, ovenproof frying pan over a medium heat. Add the onions and fry gently for a minute or two. Add courgette and fry for another two minutes. Pour in the egg mixture, stirring gently to make sure the courgette slices are spread evenly.

3. Scatter over the feta and mint and cook for another four to five minutes on the stovetop (by which stage the egg mixture should set and brown on the bottom). Finish under the grill for three or four minutes, until lightly browned and fluffy. Serve immediately.

Pasta with Tomato & Vodka Sauce

MARIE MCGUIRK, LOUTH: COOKERY TUTOR AND ASPIRING GOLFER

This simple twist on a basic tomato sauce makes an interesting change. The base sauce itself is very versatile. You could leave out the vodka if cooking for the family, and sharpen with a little lemon juice instead. Or you could add some meat of choice to flesh it out.

Serves 4–6
- 1 tablespoon extra virgin olive oil
- 2 garlic cloves, sliced
- 1 small onion or 2 shallots, very finely chopped
- 200ml (7fl oz) good quality tomato passata
- 1 handful fresh basil leaves
- 500g (1lb) dried pasta (try penne, fusilli or farfalle)
- 200ml (7fl oz) low fat crème fraîche (optional)
- 1 shot vodka
- salt and freshly ground black pepper

to serve
- 3 tablespoons freshly grated Parmesan cheese

1. Heat the olive oil in a small saucepan and gently fry the onion and garlic until soft. Add the tomato passata, season and tear in half of the basil leaves. Cook gently for about 10 minutes.

2. While the sauce is simmering, bring a large pan of salted water to the boil and cook the pasta until al dente. Drain well, reserving a little of the starchy cooking water.

3. Keeping the heat high, toss the pasta in the pan with a spatula as you add the tomato sauce and crème fraîche, if using. Add the measure of vodka, toss again and turn the heat off. Season to taste.

4. Sprinkle with Parmesan cheese and the remaining basil. Serve immediately.

ICA Tip
Usually when we cook with wine, we aim to boil off the alcohol. However if the vodka cooks and evaporates, you will lose the taste of it.

Vegetable Crumble

NORAH MCDERMOTT, KILDARE: FAN OF SAVOURY FOODS

*This was my father's speciality and was cooked on a regular basis in the house.
It is both simple and cheap to cook and the ingredients are easy to come by.
Delicious hot and cold, this is a good one for family members who
are reluctant to eat vegetables.*

Serves 4
- 2 tablespoons oil
- 2 medium onions, chopped
- 2 medium carrots, peeled and diced
- 1 large parsnip, peeled and diced
- 1 turnip, peeled and diced
- 2 tablespoons tomato purée
- 2 tablespoons horseradish sauce
- 500ml (1 pint) vegetable stock

for the crumble
- 50g (2oz) margarine
- 2 handfuls walnuts, crushed
- 2 tablespoons sesame seeds
- 1 tablespoon wheatgerm
- 2 tablespoons chopped fresh parsley

1. Preheat oven to 180°C/350°F/Gas 4.

2. Heat the oil in a large heavy-based pot and sauté the diced vegetables over a medium heat for five minutes.

3. Stir in the tomato purée and horseradish sauce. Pour the stock over, bring to the boil and allow to simmer for a minute or two. Pour into a shallow baking dish, cover with foil and bake in preheated oven for a few minutes.

4. Meanwhile sauté the crushed walnuts in the margarine with the sesame seeds and wheatgerm for two or three minutes. Mix in the parsley and place on top of the vegetables.

5. Return to oven for a further 20–30 minutes and serve with mashed potatoes.

Butterbean & Vegetable Au Gratin

AUDREY STARRETT, DONEGAL: JACK OF ALL TRADES

This recipe came about because a member of my family is a vegetarian and I often had to prepare alternative meat-free dishes. Extra portions of this meal would be used as a second vegetable for the main family meal.

Serves 6
- 40g (1½oz) butter
- 2 tablespoons oil
- 1 large onion, chopped
- 1 large carrot, diced
- ½ small turnip, diced
- 4 celery sticks, diced
- 1 tablespoon flour
- 250ml (½ pint) milk, plus extra if needed
- 400g (14oz) cooked butterbeans
- salt and freshly ground black pepper
- 110g (4oz) grated cheese
- 110g (4oz) whole-wheat breadcrumbs

to serve
- mashed potatoes
- salad

1. Heat the butter and oil in a heavy-based saucepan and sweat the onion for about five minutes or until softened. Add the carrot, turnip and celery, cover and sweat them in their own juices for about 10 minutes or until tender.

2. Preheat the grill to hot. Stir in the flour to coat the softened vegetables and cook for a minute or two. Add the milk and stir until thickened, adding more milk if you need it.

3. Add the butterbeans, season and check for taste. You can either add half the cheese to the sauce for extra flavour or reserve it all for the topping. Turn into casserole dish and sprinkle the top with mixed grated cheese and breadcrumbs.

4. Finish under preheated grill until golden brown and serve with potatoes and salad.

Mushroom Stroganoff

NORAH MCDERMOTT, KILDARE: FAN OF SAVOURY FOODS

Both my mother and my father loved to cook this recipe – it was one of my father's favourites. Not only is it a very easy dish to cook, it is very affordable and is based on easy-to-find ingredients. It's a great dish for a cold winter's day and never fails to satisfy in my family.

Serves 4
- 2 tablespoons olive oil
- 25g (1oz) butter
- 450g (1lb) mixed mushrooms (chestnut, oyster, etc)
- 2–3 tablespoons brandy, dry sherry (or apple juice)
- 1 large red onion, peeled and finely chopped
- 1 tablespoon paprika
- 250ml (½ pint) vegetable stock
- 25g (1oz) creamed coconut, grated or chopped
- 200ml (7 fl oz) crème fraîche or double cream
- salt and freshly ground black pepper
- 1 tablespoon chopped fresh parsley

to serve
- nutty brown rice

1. Heat half the oil and half the butter in a frying pan and fry the mushrooms over a high heat, tossing periodically to get a nice even colour. Add the brandy or sherry and if you're feeling flamboyant, ignite and flambé (watch those eyebrows and lashes). Transfer to a dish and keep warm.

2. Heat the remaining oil and butter over a medium heat, add the onion and fry for a few minutes. Stir in the paprika, cook for 30 seconds to release some of the aromas and add the vegetable stock and coconut. Bring to the boil and reduce by a third. Stir in the crème fraîche or double cream and continue to reduce until rich and creamy.

3. Return the mushrooms to the pan, taste and adjust the seasoning and stir in some freshly chopped parsley to finish. Serve over nutty brown rice.

ICA Tip
Brown rice is a great source of fibre.
Just simmer for 40–50 minutes in
plenty of salted water, skimming
any foam that rises to the surface.

Fish Burgers with Tartare Sauce

MARIE MCGUIRK, LOUTH: COOKERY TUTOR AND ASPIRING GOLFER

Who doesn't love burgers? Kids certainly do, making this a handy way to convince them to eat fish, should they need convincing. You may want to leave the capers out, or you could add aromatic herbs like dill or tarragon.

Makes 4 large burgers
- 450g (1lb) firm white fish, skinned and boned
- 2 teaspoons French mustard
- 2 spring onions (or 1 shallot), finely chopped
- 2 teaspoons capers, chopped (optional)
- 1 tablespoon chopped fresh parsley
- salt and freshly ground black pepper
- 2 tablespoons flour
- 1–2 tablespoons vegetable oil

for the tartare sauce
- 3–4 tablespoons good quality mayonnaise
- 2 teaspoons capers, rinsed and chopped finely
- 2 teaspoons finely chopped parsley
- 1 small shallot, chopped finely
- 1 gherkin, chopped finely (optional)
- ¼ lemon, juice only

to serve
- 4 wholemeal baps, halved
- 2 large tomatoes, sliced
- 2 handful fresh leaves

1. Finely chop the fish and combine with mustard, onions, capers and parsley in a bowl. Mix well, season and divide the mixture in four. On a lightly floured surface, shape the fish into four patties. Refrigerate for one hour.

2. Heat the oil in a fry pan and add the burgers. Gently cook for three to four minutes on each side, until the soft mixture firms up and the outside turns a nice golden brown.

3. Meanwhile, mix together the tartare sauce ingredients, adding lemon to taste. Toast the baps, spread with tartare sauce and place a fish burger on each one together with some leaves and sliced tomato.

Blackened Cajun Salmon & Citrus Yoghurt

BREDA MCDONALD, KILKENNY: PASSIONATE BELIEVER IN LOCAL COMMUNITY

This is a simple but very effective way to liven up salmon, and all the components can be prepared well in advance, making it ideal for entertaining.
You could try substituting with other oily fish such as trout or experiment with white fish like hake, and could serve with baked or steamed potatoes.

Serves 4
- 2 teaspoons Cajun spices
- 1 tablespoon chopped fresh mixed herbs (parsley, mint, thyme, oregano)
- 1 tablespoon oil
- 1 lime, zest only
- 4 salmon fillets
- 2 whole chillies, deseeded and chopped (optional)
- ½ lemon, cut into wedges

for the citrus yoghurt
- 250ml (8fl oz) natural yoghurt
- 1 tablespoon freshly chopped mint
- 1 lime, juice only
- freshly ground black pepper

to serve
- Spiced Couscous Salad (see p97 for recipe)

1. In a small bowl mix together the Cajun spices, mixed herbs and oil. Add the lime zest and salmon fillets and mix well. If time allows, leave the salmon to marinate in the fridge for 20 minutes or longer, to let the flavours develop.

2. Meanwhile to prepare the yoghurt dressing, combine the yoghurt, lime juice and freshly chopped mint in a small mixing bowl and season generously with black pepper. Refrigerate until ready to serve. Prepare the couscous salad, if using (see p97).

3. Preheat oven to 190°C/375°F/Gas 5. Line a baking tray with some parchment paper.

4. Heat a large pan with a little oil and pan-fry the salmon flesh-side down for two to three minutes to give the flesh a nice blackened effect. Transfer to the lined baking tray, sprinkle with chopped chillies and lemon wedges and bake in preheated oven for about 15 minutes or until the salmon feels firm to the touch.

5. Transfer to individual serving plates, drizzle generously with the citrus yoghurt dressing and serve immediately with salad, potatoes or couscous.

Express Fish Pie

RITA CLOHESSY, CORK: SEA-LOVING GRANDMOTHER AND FISHERWOMAN

My heart-warming nutritious fish pie can be prepared in 20 minutes, and can be easily doubled in quantity for a larger crowd. I've given the recipe to my granddaughter who has passed it on to all her friends – they say it reminds them of home.

Serves 6

- 300g (10oz) white fish, skinned and pin-boned
- 175g (6oz) smoked fish (such as haddock)
- 2–3 tablespoons butter
- ½ pint milk
- 1 small bag of frozen prawns
- 1 small bag of frozen peas
- 10–12 potatoes, peeled and quartered
- salt and freshly ground black pepper
- 1 tablespoon oil
- 1 small onion, finely chopped
- 1 heaped teaspoon cornflour
- 1 tablespoon chopped fresh parsley
- 1 tablespoon chopped fresh tarragon or dill (optional)
- 1–2 tablespoons cream (optional)

1. Put both fish in microwave dish with a knob of butter and a splash of milk, cook on high for three minutes and allow to stand. Put prawns in bowl, cover with boiling water and set aside. Preheat oven to 220°C/425°F/Gas 7.

2. Cook the potatoes at a rolling boil in lots of salted water until just tender, mash with butter and a little milk or cream and season to taste.

3. To make the sauce, heat a little oil in a frying pan over a medium heat and gently sweat the onions for about five minutes or until softened. Meanwhile, heat the remaining milk and a knob of butter in a saucepan and bring to the boil. Mix the cornflour to a smooth paste with a little water and add to the hot milk to thicken. Stir in the onion and chopped herbs, season to taste and add cream, if using.

4. Flake fish into large chunks, checking for any remaining bones. Combine in an ovenproof dish with prawns and frozen peas. Pour over sauce and pipe or spread the mashed potatoes over the top. Bake in a preheated oven for 30–40 minutes, or until golden brown.

Smoked Haddock Pie

UNA FLYNN, WESTMEATH: LOVES TO WALK THE ROYAL CANAL

I sourced this recipe from a chef over 20 years ago and have made a few alterations to it over the years to put my own stamp on it. I often cook it for get-togethers and the quantities can easily be doubled.

Serves 6–8
- 675g (1½lb) potatoes, peeled and chopped into even chunks
- 900g (2lb) smoked haddock, skinned and boned
- 1 lemon, cut into wedges
- 1 bay leaf
- 3 small onions, peeled
- 3 tomatoes, cored and chopped
- 3 hard-boiled eggs, roughly chopped
- 1 teaspoon chopped fresh parsley
- salt and freshly ground black pepper
- 1 egg, beaten

for the sauce
- 225g (8oz) butter
- 110g (4oz) flour
- 250ml (½ pint) milk
- 150ml (¼ pint) cream

to garnish
- remaining wedges of lemon
- 1 handful fresh parsley, chopped

1. Preheat oven to 190°C/375°F/Gas 5. Grease a large pie dish.

2. Bring a large pan of salted water to the boil and cook potatoes at a gentle boil until tender, about 15 minutes.

3. Meanwhile, cut fish into bite-sized pieces. Place in a saucepan with bay leaf, a couple of wedges of lemon and one onion, halved. Cover with cold water, bring to the boil and poach for eight to ten minutes. Remove fish, drain and set aside. Transfer the poaching liquid to a measuring jug and set aside.

4. Mash the cooked potato with a generous knob of butter and a splash of milk or cream and season to taste. Finely chop the remaining onions.

5. To make the sauce, melt the butter over a low heat, stir in the flour and cook for two minutes. Top up the reserved poaching water with milk and cream. You can vary the ratio depending on how rich you'd like it, but you'll need about a pint of liquid altogether. Add this liquid to the saucepan and bring to the boil, stirring continuously. Cook for one minute before reducing the heat and adding chopped onions. Simmer for a couple of minutes, remove from the heat and season to taste.

6. Stir in chopped tomatoes, eggs, parsley and fish and transfer to a greased pie dish. Pipe a border of potato around the dish, brush with beaten egg and bake in preheated oven for 30 minutes.

7. Garnish with lemon and parsley and serve hot.

Whole Baked Salmon

ANNE GABBETT, LIMERICK: DAIRY FARMER'S WIFE AND HOME ECONOMICS TEACHER

A quick, easy dish to make and delicious when served, this is also nicely affordable if cooking for a crowd. Leftover salmon keeps well in the fridge and is very versatile for sandwiches and salads.

Serves 8–10
- 1 whole salmon (about 2kg or 4½lb), cleaned, trimmed and descaled
- 4–5 shallots, peeled and quartered
- ½ bunch fresh fine herbs (dill, fennel or tarragon all work)
- 1 tablespoon butter
- salt and ground white pepper
- 150ml (¼ pint) white wine
- 250ml (½ pint) double cream
- ½ lemon, juice only

to garnish
- sprigs of fresh parsley
- slices of lemon

ICA Tip
Ask your fishmonger to clean, trim and descale the whole fish for you – that's what he's there for!

1. Preheat oven to 180°C/350°F/Gas 4.

2. Place the quartered shallot and herbs in the salmon cavity and transfer to a well-buttered ovenproof dish. Dot the fish with butter, season and pour over the wine. Cover with foil and bake in preheated oven for about an hour (or 15 minutes to the pound), basting with the cooking liquid from time to time. Pour over the cream about 20 minutes before the end of cooking.

3. To check if the fish is cooked, pierce the skin and flesh with a knife – it should be almost fully opaque but still nicely moist. Don't forget that the flesh will continue to cook after being removed from the oven. Once just cooked, transfer the salmon to a serving platter and keep warm.

4. Strain the liquid into a saucepan and reduce slightly, stirring all the time. Add the lemon juice, heat through and pour a little over the salmon. Serve the remainder separately in a sauceboat. Garnish the salmon with extra sprigs of parsley and lemon slices.

Roast Cod Steaks with Herb Pesto

LIZ WALL, WICKLOW: BUSY MUM AND ICA NATIONAL PRESIDENT

This is an extremely straightforward way of cooking a white fish such as cod, and a good example of just how easy fish can be to cook. You could substitute with a local Irish fish such as hake or halibut, both of which have beautiful white flesh.

Serves 4–6
- 4–6 portions of cod fillet, about 3cm (1¼in) thick
- salt and freshly ground black pepper
- 3 tablespoons fresh parsley, finely chopped
- 1 tablespoon each fresh dill and tarragon, finely chopped (optional)
- 2 cloves garlic, crushed with a little salt
- ½ lemon, juice and finely grated zest
- 2 tablespoons olive oil

to serve
- lemon wedges
- steamed new potatoes
- salad or vegetables

1. Preheat oven to 220°C/425°F/Gas 7.

2. Season the cod, heat a frying pan to smoking hot and add a little oil. Sear the cod for one minute on either side.

3. Transfer to a shallow, ovenproof dish and bake in preheated oven for 20–25 minutes until just cooked through.

4. Meanwhile, blitz the herbs, garlic and lemon zest with the olive oil. Season with salt, pepper and lemon juice to taste.

5. Serve with steamed new potatoes and salad or vegetables of choice, and herb pesto on the side.

Pan-Fried Hake with Salsa Verde

MARIE MCGUIRK, LOUTH: COOKERY TUTOR AND ASPIRING GOLFER

A firm white fish that is plentiful in Irish waters, hake is such an easy fish to cook. Served here with a fresh tasting salsa verde, it is as delicious as it is healthy.

Serves 4
- 4 portions of hake fillet, skinned and boned
- 2 tablespoons plain flour
- salt and freshly ground black pepper
- 2 tablespoons rapeseed oil

for the salsa verde
- 1 handful each fresh parsley, basil and mint, chopped
- 4 anchovy fillets (optional)
- 2 tablespoons capers, thoroughly rinsed
- 2 garlic cloves
- 1 tablespoon red or white wine vinegar
- 1 tablespoon caster sugar
- 1 slice white bread, crusts removed
- 150ml (¼ pint) olive oil
- salt and freshly ground black pepper

to serve
- lemon wedges
- new potatoes
- green vegetables

1. To make the salsa verde, combine all the ingredients in a food processor and whizz together. Refrigerate until fish is cooked.

2. Place the fish in a plastic bag along with the flour seasoned with salt and pepper. Shake well to coat the fish with flour.

3. Heat the oil in a frying pan and when hot, add the fish flesh-side first. Fry over a high heat for a couple of minutes to brown and crisp. Turn over, reduce the heat and continue to cook at a slower heat to ensure that the fish cooks through. This should take another three to four minutes but will depend on the thickness of the fillet. To check, press a knife into the fish which should be opaque. Take care not to overcook as the fish will dry out, and remember that it will continue to cook even when removed from the pan.

4. Serve with the salsa verde and garnish with lemon wedges. New potatoes and green vegetables make lovely healthy accompaniments.

ICA Tip
Most capers are preserved in vinegar and just need to be rinsed well. If using salted capers, you'll need to soak them for a couple of hours before use.

Pork & Potato Cakes

MARIE MCGUIRK, LOUTH: COOKERY TUTOR AND ASPIRING GOLFER

This makes for a very affordable family dinner, being based on leftover mashed potato and minced pork. There's nothing too pungent in the flavours either, making it attractive to kids who tend to appreciate the sweetness the apple brings.

Serves 4
- 225g (8oz) minced pork
- 450g (1lb) mashed potatoes
- 1 small cooking apple, grated
- ½ small onion, chopped
- 2 teaspoons chopped sage leaves
- salt and freshly ground black pepper
- 1 tablespoon flour
- 1 tablespoon rapeseed oil
- 2 sweet red apples, cored and sliced into thin wedges

to garnish
- sage leaves

1. Mix together the pork, potato, apple, onion and sage. Season, sprinkle a little flour on a clean surface and divide the pork into eight even portions. Shape the portions into round cakes, cover and refrigerate for 15 minutes.

2. Heat the oil in a non-stick frying pan and cook the cakes over a low to medium heat for about 15 minutes, turning periodically to prevent burning. After 10 minutes, add the apple wedges and cook until softened.

3. Serve two cakes per portion garnished with fried apple wedges and sage leaves. Alternatively you could serve these between two baps in place of a burger.

ICA Tip
Try frying the sage leaves in a little butter and oil to crisp them up before garnishing.

Dublin Coddle

MAUREEN BUTLER, MEATH: BRIDGE-PLAYING MOTHER OF FOUR

As a child growing up in Dublin, we always had this served to us at the end of the week when all that was left were rashers, sausages and potatoes. Everything was put into the one pot and cooked. It was delicious, particularly on a cold winter's day.

Serves 6
- 2kg (4½lb) potatoes, peeled
- 500ml (1 pint) boiled water
- 1 ham, chicken or beef stock cube (optional)
- 450g (1lb) good quality pork sausages
- 450g (1lb) piece thick-cut bacon
- 2 large onions, sliced
- 1 tablespoon finely chopped fresh parsley
- salt and coarse ground pepper

to serve
- fresh soda bread

ICA Tip
Pork sausages are best bought from a local butcher.

1. Preheat oven to 150°C/300°F/Gas 2.

2. Cut any larger potatoes into three or four pieces, leaving smaller ones whole so that they will cook evenly. Dissolve the stock cube in the boiled water, if using.

3. Grill the sausages and bacon long enough to colour them but taking care not to dry them out. Drain on paper towels and chop the bacon into 2½cm (1in) pieces. You can chop the sausages into bite-sized pieces, though some prefer to leave them whole.

4. In a large ovenproof casserole dish with a tight lid, layer the onions, bacon, sausages and potatoes, seasoning each layer liberally with pepper and parsley. Continue until the ingredients are used up and pour the hot water or bouillon mixture over the top.

5. On the stove, bring the liquid to a boil. Immediately reduce heat and cover the pot. You may like to put a layer of foil underneath the pot lid to help seal it.

6. Place the covered pot in preheated oven and cook for at least three hours (up to four or five hours will not hurt it). After two hours, check liquid levels and add more water if necessary. There should be about an inch of liquid at the bottom of the pot at all times.

7. Serve hot with fresh soda bread to mop up the lovely gravy.

Pork Chops & Bubble 'n' Leek Cakes

ADA VANCE, CAVAN: HILL-WALKING GRANNY AND EXPERT PATCHWORKER

This dish of mine was always a favourite in our house. I entered it into a local cookery competition that Neven Maguire was judging and it won. I was just thrilled to have done so well.

Serves 4
- 4 pork loin chops
- 1 tablespoon English mustard
- 1 tablespoon picked fresh thyme leaves

For the bubble 'n' leek cakes
- 1kg (2.2lb) potatoes, peeled and diced large
- 50g (2oz) butter
- 1 medium leek, sliced
- salt and freshly ground black pepper
- 4 tablespoons flour
- 3 tablespoons oil

1. Preheat oven to 220°C/425°F/Gas 7. Brush pork chops with mustard, press on thyme leaves and cook on a preheated baking tray for 30 minutes or until cooked through and golden.

2. Meanwhile, gently boil potatoes in a large pan of salted water for 10–12 minutes or until just tender. Drain, return to the pan and allow to steam for two minutes before mashing until smooth.

3. Melt butter in a large frying pan over a medium to low heat. Gently sweat leeks until soft and melting, about 10 minutes. Stir into mash, season and form into eight cakes. Season the flour and dust each potato cake in it.

4. Once the pork chops are cooked through, set aside somewhere warm to rest while you cook off your potato cakes. Heat oil in a non-stick frying pan and cook cakes for two minutes on each side or until golden and crisp at the edges. Serve immediately with pork chops.

Chicken & Vegetable Stir-Fry

AN GRIANÁN, LOUTH: ICA ADULT EDUCATION CENTRE

The key to a good stir-fry is marinating the meat and thinking about the order the vegetables should be cooked in. You could give the broccoli a little head-start by blanching it first. Feel free to add whatever vegetables are in your fridge and take your fancy.

Serves 4
- 4 chicken fillets
- 1 garlic clove, crushed
- ½cm (¼in) piece of ginger, peeled and grated (optional)
- 2 tablespoons soy sauce
- 2 tablespoons vegetable oil
- ½ head broccoli, cut into small florets
- ½ yellow, red or orange pepper, deseeded and cut into strips
- 2 small carrots, peeled and cut into thin batons
- 2 handfuls French beans, mange tout or sugar snaps, trimmed

to serve
- steamed basmati or Jasmine rice
- 1 tablespoon sesame seeds, lightly toasted (optional)

1. Chop chicken fillets into even bite-size strips and marinate in soy sauce, garlic and ginger for a few hours or overnight in the fridge.

2. To blanch any vegetables which require a little more cooking, such as the broccoli, simply immerse in a pan of salted water, bring to the boil and cook at a simmer for a minute or two. Transfer to cold water to arrest the cooking and drain well.

3. Heat a tablespoon of oil in a heavy frying-pan or wok and fry the chicken pieces for 10 minutes. Remove from pan and keep warm.

4. Add another tablespoon of oil and stir-fry the vegetables until cooked but still a little al dente. Think about what order to add each to the wok, depending on how thick they're cut and how cooked you'd like them to be.

5. Combine the vegetables and chicken and serve with steamed rice. If you like you could lightly toast some sesame seeds in a dry pan and scatter these over to garnish.

Fragrant Chicken Curry

MARIE MCGUIRK, LOUTH: COOKERY TUTOR AND ASPIRING GOLFER

Mild in terms of chilli heat but full-flavoured with aromatic spices, this creamy curry makes a great addition to any repertoire of speedy supper dishes.

Serves 4–6
- 4 large skinless chicken fillets, cut into chunks
- 3 tablespoons vegetable oil
- 1 tablespoon yellow or brown mustard seeds
- 1 large onion, sliced
- 3 garlic cloves, finely sliced
- 400ml (¾ pint) coconut milk
- 110g (4oz) spinach
- salt and freshly ground black pepper

for the marinade
- 1½ tablespoons ground coriander seeds
- 1 teaspoon ground cumin
- 1 teaspoon cayenne pepper
- 1 teaspoon paprika
- ½ teaspoon turmeric
- ½ teaspoon salt
- 1 tablespoon lemon juice
- 80ml (3fl oz) water

to serve
- rice or naan bread

1. Mix together all the marinade ingredients to give you a loose, smooth paste. Add the chicken pieces and toss so they are well coated. Set aside to marinate, ideally for up to an hour in the fridge, but if you are in a hurry a few minutes will do.

2. Heat the oil in a deep frying pan over a gentle heat and add the mustard seeds. When they start to pop, add the onion and garlic and cook until golden brown, taking care not to burn the garlic.

3. Add the chicken and any extra paste from the marinade, and fry over a gentle heat for about eight minutes. Add the coconut milk, increase the heat slightly and bring to a simmer. Cook for a further ten to 12 minutes until the sauce has thickened slightly.

4. Stir in the spinach, season to taste and serve with rice or naan bread.

ICA Tip
Burnt garlic tastes bitter so take care to start the cooking on a gentle heat.

Roast Goose with Damson & Apple Sauce

BRID MALONE, LAOIS: MOTHER OF FIVE, WALKER AND SWIMMER

———————————————— 🍴 ————————————————

My mother was a plain cook but what she cooked was always delicious, including this roast goose with home-made sauce and stuffing. I often cook it for Christmas dinner, enlisting my grandchildren's help to pass on the skills. This recipe won an All Ireland Cookery Competition in 1998.

Serves 8
- 1 young goose, with giblets, about 4.5–5.5kg (10–12lb)
- salt and freshly ground black pepper
- 2–3 tablespoons flour

for the stuffing
- 225g (8oz) onion, finely chopped
- 40g (1½oz) butter
- 1 goose liver (from giblets), finely chopped
- 225g (8oz) fresh white breadcrumbs
- 1 dessertspoon chopped fresh sage
- salt and freshly ground black pepper
- 2 eggs, beaten

to serve
- Damson & Apple Sauce (p109)
- Parisian Potatoes (p93)
- Puréed Parsnips (p92)
- Puréed Brussels Sprouts (p88)

ICA Tip
Be sure to ask your butcher for the giblets, including the liver.

1. The night before, soak the damsons in cider to plump up (see p109 for full recipe).

2. Preheat oven to 220°C/425°F/Gas 7.

3. To make the stuffing, melt the butter in a saucepan and sauté the onion for five minutes. Add chopped liver and cook for a further five minutes, stirring. Mix in the breadcrumbs and sage, season and bind mixture with the eggs.

4. Place the stuffing into the tail end of goose and grip together the closure with a small skewer. Place goose on a roasting rack or trivet if you have one. Prick the flesh all over with a skewer, season well and dust thoroughly with flour. Roast in preheated oven for 30 minutes before lowering temperature to 180°C/350°F/Gas 4. Cook for a further 3½ hours, pouring the excess fat out of the roasting tin several times during the cooking and reserving it for cooking the sauce and potatoes.

5. Meanwhile, prepare the giblet stock (p110), damson and apple sauce (p109) and sides dishes of puréed parsnips (p92), puréed sprouts (p88) and Parisian potatoes (p93).

6. To serve the goose, drain it well and place on a hot serving dish. Drain off the fat from the tin, reserving for later use. Add a tablespoon of flour and cook on the stovetop, stirring, for a minute or two. Deglaze with a little of the reserved cider, stirring well, and add some giblet stock. Season and simmer for a few minutes to make a glossy gravy.

7. Carve the goose at the table and serve with stuffing and damson sauce on the side, along with side dishes of puréed parsnips, puréed sprouts and Parisian potatoes.

Rabbit Pie

MARIE MCGUIRK, LOUTH: COOKERY TUTOR AND ASPIRING GOLFER

This very traditional pie featured as one of the challenges in RTE's ICA Bootcamp. Its preparation may not be for the faint-hearted, although your butcher will do the skinning, boning and dicing of the rabbit if you ask him nicely. The results will be no less impressive.

Serves 6–8
- 500g (1lb) puff pastry (use ready-made or see recipe, p135)
- 1 egg, beaten

for the pie filling
- 2 rabbits, or about 750g (1½lb) rabbit meat, skinned, boned and meat diced
- 50g (2oz) flour
- salt and freshly ground black pepper
- 25g (1oz) butter
- 2–3 tablespoons sunflower oil
- 8 shallots, peeled and cut in half
- 1 red pepper, deseeded and diced
- 2 celery sticks, diced
- 225g (8oz) button mushrooms, wiped and cut into quarters
- 1 large glass white wine
- 1 chicken stock cube
- 2 teaspoons chopped fresh thyme
- 2 tablespoons chopped fresh parsley
- 200g (7oz) crème fraîche

1. Preheat oven to 200°C/400°F/Gas 6.

2. In a mixing bowl, season the flour with a little salt and pepper, add the diced rabbit meat and toss to coat well. Melt the butter in a splash of oil in a heavy-based frying pan and brown the meat over a high heat in batches, transferring each batch to a large casserole dish as you go.

3. When all the meat is browned, add some more oil to the pan and toss the shallots, peppers, celery and mushrooms over a medium heat for five minutes. Add the vegetables to the browned meat.

4. Dissolve the stock cube in a little hot water and stir into the casserole dish with the wine. Top up with enough water to come three quarters of the way up the meat, add thyme and stir well. Cover and cook in preheated oven for one hour or until the meat is cooked. Stir in the crème fraîche and parsley and allow to cool a little in order to add the pastry lid.

5. Roll out the pastry slightly larger than the casserole dish. Place a ramekin dish upside-down in the middle of the casserole (or use a traditional pie-funnel if you have one). Trim the edges of the pastry and reform these trimmings into a border of pastry for the edge of the casserole dish, brushing the dish with cold water to help the pastry stick. Brush the pastry edge with water and place the rolled out sheet of pastry on top. The ramekin will prevent this pastry lid from sinking in the middle.

6. Seal the edges well, crimping with fingers, a fork or the back of a knife to give a nice finish. Brush with beaten egg and return to oven for 20 minutes to puff pastry. Reduce the heat to 180°C/350°F/Gas 4 and cook for a further 10–15 mins or until the pastry is well cooked and the filling piping hot.

Roast Chicken with Onion & Thyme Stuffing

GWEN CARTER, WESTMEATH: BELOVED MOTHER AND GRANDMOTHER, RIP

A really easy recipe with great results guaranteed. Gwen passed away in July 2011 but her family kindly allowed us to use this recipe, which was what she always treated any ICA visitors to when we were down with her.

Serves 4–6
- 1 medium chicken, approximately 1.5kg (3½lb)
- 1 onion, roughly chopped
- 2–3 tablespoons olive oil
- salt and freshly ground black pepper

for the stuffing
- 100g (4oz) bread, broken into pieces
- 1 tablespoon chopped fresh parsley
- 1 tablespoon chopped fresh thyme
- 1 small onion, peeled and quartered
- 50g (2oz) butter, softened

for the gravy
- 1 tablespoon flour
- 400ml (¾ pint) chicken stock (home-made if possible, see p111)

to serve
- Granny's Roast Potatoes (see p96)

ICA Tip

Be sure to reserve the chicken carcass and make your own stock. See p111 for instructions. It's a great habit to get into.

1. Preheat oven to 200°C/400°F/Gas 6.

2. To make the stuffing, combine the bread, herbs and onion in a food processor. Blitz until you have fine breadcrumbs and the onion is finely chopped. Season, add the butter and give it another quick blitz. Pack the stuffing into the body cavity of the chicken and fold over any loose skin to close. Secure with a cocktail stick.

3. Place the chicken in a roasting tin. Drizzle with olive oil and season well with salt and pepper. Place in the centre of preheated oven and roast for ten minutes. Reduce the heat to 180°C/350°F/Gas 4 and roast for about 80 mins (allowing 20 minutes per 450g/1lb, plus an extra 20 minutes).

4. Halfway through cooking, spoon the juices over the chicken and add a couple of tablespoons of water to the roasting tin to stop it from burning. At this point, you can also add the tray of parboiled roast potatoes to roast on a lower shelf (see p96).

5. To check if the chicken is cooked, pierce the thickest part of the leg: the juices should run clear. When fully cooked remove the chicken from the oven, transfer to a carving board and cover loosely with foil. Allow to rest in a warm place for 10 minutes while you make the gravy. Check if the potatoes are cooked, you may need to increase the heat to give them a final blast while the chicken is resting.

6. Strain all but one tablespoon of fat from the roast chicken tin. Sprinkle in the flour and cook in the baking tray on the stovetop, stirring, for a couple of minutes before adding stock. Bring to the boil, stirring and scraping to loosen the caramelised meat juices. Simmer for two to three minutes, season to taste and strain into a gravy boat.

7. Serve slices of roast chicken with the onion and thyme stuffing, gravy and roast potatoes.

Turkey Meatballs with Pasta

MARIE MCGUIRK, LOUTH: COOKERY TUTOR AND ASPIRING GOLFER

Turkey's not just for Christmas you know. This quick and easy family meal makes a nice change from traditional meatballs or chicken pasta dishes, and the turkey meat has enough flavour to stand up to the tomato sauce.

Serves 4–6
- 450g (1lb) minced turkey
- 1 onion, very finely chopped
- 2 garlic cloves, crushed
- 50g (2oz) fresh breadcrumbs
- salt and freshly ground black pepper
- 1 tablespoon oil
- 1 red pepper, sliced
- 400g (14oz) tinned tomatoes with herbs
- 1 carrot, grated
- pinch of chilli flakes (optional)
- 150ml (¼ pint) stock or water
- 350g (12oz) dried pasta

to serve
- 1 handful fresh basil leaves, torn
- 2 tablespoons freshly grated Parmesan (optional)

1. Combine the turkey in a mixing bowl with half the onion and half the garlic. Add the breadcrumbs, mix well and season. With damp hands, form the mixture into small balls about the size of a golf ball and chill while you prepare the sauce.

2. Heat the oil in a heavy-based saucepan over a medium heat and sweat the remaining onion and garlic with the red pepper for five minutes or until softened. Add the tomatoes, grated carrot and chilli, if using, and top up with stock or water.

3. Heat through, add the turkey meatballs into the sauce and cover with a lid. Simmer gently for 20 minutes, adding more stock or water if the sauce becomes very thick. Season to taste.

4. Cook the pasta according to packet instructions and drain. Divide between four bowls and serve the meatballs and sauce on top. Scatter with some torn basil leaves and a little grated Parmesan if using.

ICA Tip
Adding a couple of tablespoons of the starchy cooking water to the sauce will help it bind to the pasta.

HOW TO COOK WITHIN A BUDGET

1. Cooking seasonally and buying locally can be a good way to cut down on transportation costs, particularly as the price of fuel continues to rise.

2. Where possible, find a way to re-use rather than discard. Stale bread has many uses, from sweet puddings to savoury casings.

3. Ask your butcher to recommend cheaper cuts of meat and poultry (like pork belly, beef shin or chicken leg). Season these well and cook slowly for delicious results.

4. Talk to your fishmonger and be willing to experiment with fish you haven't cooked before.

5. Learn to use every bit of the animal or at least as much as is good to use. Buying a whole chicken is cheaper in the long run than buying the premium chicken fillets.

6. Save the cooking water drained from potatoes and vegetables and reuse as a light stock for soups and gravies – the best of the nutrients are in there.

7. Make your own stocks from leftover bones and vegetable trimmings.

8. Grow your own fruit and vegetables, or at the very least try growing your own herbs.

9. Buy what you really need, not what you think you'll need. We waste one third of the food we buy today. Double check 'use-by' dates when shopping, but use your instinct – and your senses – with 'best before' dates.

10. Use your freezer well and wisely. All sorts of foods can be successfully frozen, from pastry to leftover herbs chopped into ice-cubes. Beware however of forgetting what you have in there. Always label clearly and include the date.

Pork & Cider Stroganoff

EDWARD HAYDEN, KILKENNY: TV CHEF AND FOOD WRITER

This winning dish is very quick to prepare. You could forego the cider and replace with extra stock or an unsweetened apple juice. Once cooked, it could also be transferred to a casserole dish, topped with short crust or rough puff pastry and baked in a hot oven for 20 minutes.

Serves 6

- 2 pork steaks, about 450g (1lb) each, trimmed
- 25g (1oz) butter
- salt and freshly ground black pepper
- 1 large onion, diced roughly
- 8 mushrooms, wiped and sliced
- 25g (1oz) flour
- ½ teaspoon paprika or cayenne pepper
- 330ml (11fl oz) cider
- 100ml (3½fl oz) pouring cream
- 400ml (¾ pint) vegetable or chicken stock (see p111 for recipe)
- 1–2 tablespoons wholegrain mustard
- 1 large cooking apple, cored and diced
- 2 tablespoons chopped fresh parsley

1. Melt the butter in a large heavy-based saucepan over a medium heat, adding a little oil to prevent the butter from burning. Dice pork into bite-sized pieces and cook in the butter, tossing for a few minutes to seal the pork all over.

2. Season and add onions and mushrooms and cook gently for a couple of minutes. Combine the flour and paprika. Remove the saucepan from the heat and stir in the seasoned flour, taking care to coat the pork and vegetables well. Return the saucepan to the heat, pour in the cider, cream and stock, and stir in the wholegrain mustard.

3. Allow the sauce to come to the boil before adding the apple. Reduce the heat and cook at a gentle simmer for a further 30–35 minutes. Stir in freshly chopped parsley just before serving, and serve with steamed basmati rice.

ICA Tip
Begin by preparing all of your ingredients – you will need to stand over this dish for the first few minutes of cooking.

Hungarian Beef Goulash

EDWARD HAYDEN, KILKENNY: TV CHEF AND FOOD WRITER

As with most stews, this tastes even better the next day when the flavours have had time to develop. This makes it an ideal choice for home entertaining when cooking in advance can take the pressure off.

Serves 4–6
- 700g (1½lb) stewing beef (see Tip)
- 2 tablespoons oil
- 1 large onion, diced
- 6 garlic cloves, roughly chopped
- 2 carrots, diced
- 1 red or green pepper, deseeded and diced
- 2 teaspoons paprika
- 1 tablespoon flour
- 2 teaspoons tomato purée
- dash of Worcestershire sauce (optional)
- ½ glass red wine
- 400g (14oz) chopped tomatoes (tinned is fine)
- 2 tablespoons sour cream
- 500ml (1 pint) beef stock

to serve
- boiled rice or crusty rolls

1. Trim the beef of fat and cut the meat into large bite-sized chunks. Heat some oil in a large heavy-based saucepan or casserole and cook the diced beef over a high heat until it is browned all over.

2. Add the onion, garlic, carrot and red or green pepper and cook for a further minute or two. Combine the paprika and flour, stir into the pot and cook for a few minutes to release the spice aromas and coat the meat and vegetables.

3. Add the tomato purée and Worcestershire sauce, if using, and cook for a minute before adding the red wine and cooking for a further minute or two.

4. Stir in the tomatoes and sour cream, add the stock and allow the mixture to return to the boil. Cover with a tight-fitting lid, reduce heat and cook at a gentle simmer for 75–90 minutes or until the meat is tender.

5. Serve with some boiled rice or crusty bread rolls.

ICA Tip
Neck, chuck, shoulder and shin are all good cuts of beef for stewing, or ask your butcher for a recommendation.

Irish Stew

MARY HARRAHILL, MEATH: ENJOYS A GOOD CÉILÍ

This is my slightly modern take on one of the most traditional of Irish dishes. Irish stew used to be based on mutton and cooked for hours to tenderise, but today's lamb needs less time to cook. Ask your butcher to suggest a good stewing cut such as neck or shoulder.

Serves 4-6
- 700g (1½lb) stewing lamb, diced
- 1 litre (1¾ pints) stock (lamb, vegetable or chicken, see p111)
- 450g (1lb) potatoes
- 110g (4oz) carrots, peeled or scrubbed
- 110g (4oz) celery, trimmed
- 110g (4oz) leeks, trimmed
- 110g (4oz) white cabbage, sliced
- 1 medium onion, peeled
- 1 bouquet garni, tied together with twine (see Tip)
- 400g (14oz) cooked cannellini beans (optional)
- 1 tablespoon chopped fresh parsley
- salt and freshly ground black pepper

to serve
- warm soda bread

1. Put the lamb into a large pan, cover with stock and bring to the boil. Skim off any foam and excess fat from the top and leave to simmer for 30 minutes over a low heat while you prepare the vegetables.

2. Peel the potatoes and cut into 2.5cm (1in) dice. Cut all the vegetables into 1cm (½in) pieces. Add these to the lamb together with the potatoes and bouquet garni. Increase the heat and bring to the boil, then reduce the heat and simmer for a further 20–25 minutes until the lamb is tender.

3. Add the cooked cannellini beans and simmer for a final five minutes to heat through. Remove the bouquet garni and check seasoning. Sprinkle with chopped parsley and serve with warm soda bread.

ICA Tip
A bouquet garni is a bundle of hardy herbs like parsley, thyme and bayleaf tied with string and removed before serving.

Shepherd's Pie

CLAIRE ANN MCDONNELL, WICKLOW: LOVES GARDENING AND THE COUNTRY AIR

Shepherd's pie is traditionally made with minced lamb but I prefer to make mine with minced beef. You could do either. I like to beef up the flavour too with some storecupboard staples like brown sauce and a packet of oxtail soup, but you could add a beef stock cube instead.

Serves 4–6

- 450g (1lb) potatoes, peeled and quartered
- 450g (1lb) minced beef or lamb
- 2–3 tablespoons oil
- 1 onion, halved and sliced
- 1 large carrot, peeled and grated
- 1 handful frozen peas or French beans
- 2–3 tablespoons Worcestershire sauce
- 1 tablespoon brown sauce
- 1 packet powdered oxtail soup (or 1 beef stock cube)
- salt and freshly ground black pepper
- 50g (2oz) butter
- 1 egg, beaten
- 25g (1oz) cheddar cheese, grated

1. Preheat oven to 200°C/400°F/Gas 6.

2. In a large pan, cook the potatoes in plenty of salted water at a gentle rolling boil for 15 minutes or until just tender.

3. Meanwhile heat some oil in a heavy-based saucepan and fry the beef over a medium to high heat until browned. You might want to do this in batches to ensure it browns nicely. Add the vegetables, Worcestershire sauce, brown sauce and powdered soup or crumbled stock cube and top up with water, just enough to moisten. Season and simmer for ten minutes before transferring to an ovenproof dish.

4. Mash the cooked potatoes, add the butter and beaten egg, season to taste and mix well. Top the meat with the mashed potato, smooth over and score with a knife to help it crisp up.

5. Sprinkle lightly with grated cheese and cook on middle shelf of preheated oven for 30 minutes, or until the cheese melts and potato crispens and turns golden.

Meat Loaf

KATHLEEN GORMAN, LAOIS: BAKER, KNITTER AND KEEN READER

This is something that I created myself and is popular in my immediate family. It is delicious served hot or cold with salad as an evening meal.

Serves 4–6
- 700g (1½lb) minced beef and/or pork
- 140g (5oz) breadcrumbs
- 50g (2oz) mushrooms, chopped
- 1 onion, finely chopped
- 1 tablespoon Worcestershire sauce
- 1 egg, beaten
- 150ml (¼ pint) milk
- ½ teaspoon marjoram
- pinch of garlic powder (or ½ garlic clove, minced)
- salt and freshly ground black pepper
- 4 tablespoons tomato ketchup

You will need
- 900g (2lb) loaf tin

1. Preheat oven to 180°C/350°F/Gas 4.

2. Combine all ingredients except the tomato ketchup in a large mixing bowl and mix well.

3. Transfer the mixture to an ungreased 900g (2lb) loaf tin and spread the tomato ketchup over the top.

4. Bake in preheated oven for 60–75 minutes. Turn on to serving plate, straining off excess fat.

5. Serve hot or cold with potatoes, vegetables or salad.

Beef & Mushroom Pie

MARIE MCGUIRK, LOUTH: COOKERY TUTOR AND ASPIRING GOLFER

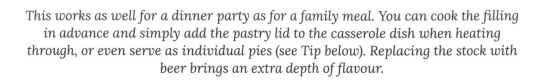

This works as well for a dinner party as for a family meal. You can cook the filling in advance and simply add the pastry lid to the casserole dish when heating through, or even serve as individual pies (see Tip below). Replacing the stock with beer brings an extra depth of flavour.

Serves 4–6
- 1kg (2lb) rib steak, trimmed and diced
- 2–3 tablespoons oil
- 1 medium onion, chopped
- 1 tablespoon flour
- 150ml (¼ pint) beef stock (or ale / beer)
- 225g (8oz) mushrooms, wiped and cut in quarters
- 2–3 tablespoons chopped fresh herbs (parsley, thyme, marjoram etc)
- 1 bay leaf
- 1 tablespoon Worcestershire sauce
- 1 teaspoon mustard
- salt and freshly ground black pepper
- 450g puff pastry (ready-made or see p135 for recipe)
- 1 egg, beaten

to serve
- green salad
- baked potatoes
- vegetables of choice

ICA Tip
Try serving the pie filling in individual ramekins. Cut out ovals of pastry and bake separately on a baking sheet, then pop them as lids onto each ramekin dish.

1. Preheat oven to 170°C/325°F/Gas 3.

2. Heat oil in a heavy-based ovenproof casserole over a medium to high heat and fry the beef to seal it, tossing to brown evenly. Add the onion and continue to cook for a few minutes. Stir in the flour and cook for another minute before gradually adding the stock or ale, stirring to avoid lumps. Add the mushrooms and bring the mixture to boiling point, stirring continuously. Finally add the herbs, Worcestershire sauce and mustard, and check seasoning.

3. Cover and transfer to preheated oven to simmer gently for about 90 minutes or until the meat is tender, stirring occasionally and adding more stock or ale if needed. Check after an hour, as the cooking time will depend on the quality of your meat. Once tender, increase the oven to 200°C/400°F/Gas 6. Remove casserole from oven and transfer the contents to a large bowl to cool a little.

4. Once cool enough to handle, place a deep ramekin dish upside-down in the centre of the casserole dish and surround with the pie filling. Roll out pastry large enough to cover the casserole dish. Wet the edges of the casserole with water to help create a seal, transfer the pastry on top and press edges to seal. The ramekin will prevent the pastry from collapsing and becoming soggy.

5. Brush pastry with beaten egg to glaze and bake in preheated oven for 25–30 minutes until well risen and golden. Serve piping hot with salad or baked potato and vegetables.

Braised Derrynaflan Brisket

LILY BARRETT, TIPPERARY: LOVES COOKING, DANCING AND VOLUNTEERING

My local butcher always had the best brisket, a cheap cut that really delivers on flavour. My mother's hotpot recipe is a great winter dish. I have been cooking it for over 40 years and renamed it after an ancient chalice that was found on Derrynaflan Island, Co Tipperary.

Serves 4
- 700g (1½lb) brisket of beef, boned and rolled
- 1 tablespoon vegetable oil
- 1 tablespoon margarine
- 1 onion, chopped finely
- 4 medium carrots, peeled and chopped
- 4 medium leeks, trimmed and sliced
- 250ml (½ pint) chicken stock (see p111)
- 2 bay leaves
- 1 sprig of thyme
- ½ glass white wine
- 1 tablespoon cornflour
- 1–2 tablespoons sour cream (optional)

to serve
- baked potatoes
- 2 handfuls grated cheddar cheese (optional)
- 2 handfuls cress (optional)

1. Preheat oven to 190°C/375°F/Gas 5.

2. In a flameproof casserole, heat the oil and margarine and brown the brisket well all over. Add the onion, cover and cook on a gentle heat for 10 minutes before transferring to preheated oven. After 45 minutes, add the carrots, leeks, stock and herbs, and continue cooking for another hour.

3. Transfer the brisket to warmed serving dish and remove the string. Remove the vegetables from the casserole with slotted spoon and arrange around the brisket.

4. Strain the cooking liquid into a small saucepan, add the wine and boil fast for five minutes. Blend the cornflour to a smooth paste in a couple of tablespoons of water, stirring out any for lumps, and add this gradually to the sauce to thicken to desired consistency. You may not need to add all the cornflour paste. Cook for another few minutes and finish with sour cream, to taste. Pour over the meat or into a sauceboat to serve separately.

5. Serve the brisket, vegetables and sauce with baked potatoes stuffed with grated cheddar cheese and topped with cress.

Crusted Rack of Lamb with Orange & Olive Salad

MARIE MCGUIRK, LOUTH: COOKERY TUTOR AND ASPIRING GOLFER

My father used to kill his own lambs on the farm and we would have an abundance of it at certain times of the year, usually late spring or autumn. This was before refrigeration, so the meat would be divided between two households. This recipe reminds me of childhood but with a modern, Mediterranean twist.

Serves 4
- 1 trimmed rack of lamb (8 cutlets)
- salt and freshly ground black pepper
- 25g (1oz) butter
- 1 tablespoon oil
- 1 shallot, finely chopped
- 1 tablespoon Dijon mustard
- 85g (3oz) fresh breadcrumbs
- 1 tablespoon finely chopped fresh parsley
- 1 tablespoon finely chopped fresh mint
- 1 orange, grated rind only

for the orange and olive salad
- 2–3 oranges
- 1 handful picked fresh parsley leaves
- 1 handful picked fresh mint leaves
- 4 generous handfuls salad leaves
- 85g (3oz) pitted black olives, halved or sliced

ICA Tip
You can vary the herbs in the crust, finely chopping hardy herbs like rosemary and thyme.

1. Preheat oven to 200°C/400°F/Gas 6.

2. Score the fat of the lamb well with a sharp knife and rub in a generous seasoning of salt and pepper. Cook on a roasting tray in preheated oven for an initial 10–15 minutes (depending on whether you like it cooked medium or well done).

3. Meanwhile melt butter in a little oil and sweat the shallot until soft and translucent. Add the breadcrumbs, parsley and orange, mix well and season to taste.

4. Remove the lamb from the oven and spread with the mustard. Taking care not to burn yourself, press the stuffing on top of the mustard and pack it down well so that it sticks to the lamb. Return the rack to the oven for another 20–25 minutes (or longer if you prefer it very well-done). You can cover loosely with foil if the crust gets too brown before lamb is cooked.

5. To make the salad, remove the orange skin and pith with a sharp knife and cut into segments. Combine in a serving bowl with the herbs, leaves and olives and drizzle over a little orange juice.

6. When the lamb is cooked to your liking, remove it from the oven and set it aside somewhere warm for five minutes to rest. Serve two cutlets per person garnished with the salad.

Fillet of Beef with Roast Shallot & Balsamic Reduction

EDWARD HAYDEN, KILKENNY: TV CHEF AND FOOD WRITER

One of the most common queries at my cookery demonstrations is how to cook the perfect steak. It is a surprisingly straightforward process: the keys being a hot pan, attention to timing and allowing the meat to rest before serving. I like to serve them with spring onion potato cakes.

Serves 6
- 6 fillet steaks, about 200g (7oz) each
- 3–4 tablespoons oil
- salt and freshly ground black pepper

for the spring onion potato cakes
- 4 large potatoes, peeled and cut into even chunks
- 50g (2oz) butter
- 1–2 tablespoons milk
- 1 bunch spring onions, thinly sliced
- 1 tablespoon chopped fresh parsley
- 3 tablespoons flour
- 1 egg yolk, beaten

for the roast shallot & balsamic reduction
- 4 shallots, thinly sliced
- 25g (1oz) brown sugar
- 150ml (5fl oz) balsamic vinegar

ICA Tip
For rare, cook two minutes on either side; for medium, four minutes on either side; for well-done, five minutes on either side. For very thick fillets, allow a little longer.

1. Preheat oven to 220°C/425°F/Gas 7.

2. To make the potato cakes, cook the potatoes in plenty of boiling salted water and mash with a little butter and milk. Allow to cool before combining with spring onions, parsley and flour. Bind with egg and mould into individual cakes.

3. Heat a large pan with a little oil and shallow fry the potato cakes until brown on either sides. Transfer to a baking tray in preheated oven for a further 10 minutes to finish.

4. Wipe the pan clean and add another slick of oil. Season the steaks with black pepper and cook in hot pan to your preference (see Tip for guide to temperatures and timings). Transfer to a warm plate, cover loosely with foil and set aside somewhere warm to rest for five minutes before serving.

5. Meanwhile add the thinly sliced shallots to the pan with a little extra oil, and cook for a few minutes over a medium heat until they begin to colour. Add the sugar and allow to melt fully before pouring in the balsamic vinegar. Bring to the boil and reduce to a syrup-like consistency.

6. Serve the steak on top of the potato cake and drizzle with the roast shallot and balsamic reduction.

Marinated Roast Fillet

MARY HARRAHILL, MEATH: ENJOYS A GOOD CÉILÍ

This is a real treat of a dish and a lovely one for a family gathering. The beef is best marinated overnight so you'll have to start the day before, but it really is a very easy recipe with impressive results.

Serves 6–8

- 1½kg (3lb) beef fillet (middle piece), well trimmed and tied
- 4 generous handfuls French beans, trimmed
- 1 punnet cherry tomatoes
- 1–2 tablespoons olive oil

for the marinade

- 2 tablespoons olive oil
- 2 garlic cloves, finely chopped
- 2 tablespoons dry sherry
- 1½cm (½in) piece of ginger, chopped
- 2 tablespoons soy sauce

for the sauce

- 125ml (4fl oz) dry white wine
- salt and freshly ground black pepper
- 4 spring onions (white part only), finely chopped

ICA Tip

Allow eight minutes per pound for rare beef and 10 minutes per pound for medium; or use a meat thermometer for precise results.

1. Place the fillet in a shallow dish. Combine the marinade ingredients, mixing well, and pour over the meat. Cover and refrigerate overnight, turning occasionally.

2. Preheat oven to 200°C/400°F/Gas 6. Transfer the meat onto a roasting tin, reserving the marinade. Roast the fillet in preheated oven for 25–30 minutes for rare to medium (or longer for well done), basting with the marinade during cooking.

3. Meanwhile, blanch the French beans. Immerse the beans in a pan of salted water, bring to the boil and simmer for three to four minutes. Drain and plunge in iced water to arrest the cooking, then pat dry. Heat a little olive oil in a frying pan and sauté the beans and tomatoes over a medium to high heat. Remove from the heat, season to taste and cover to keep warm.

4. When the meat is cooked to your preference, remove from roasting tin, wrap in foil and set aside to rest in a warm place for five minutes while you deglaze the tin with the wine. Stir over a high heat to loosen any remaining scraps of meat, gathering up the juices and adding a little water if necessary. Add spring onions and season to taste.

5. Slice the fillet and serve with the sauce and sautéed vegetables.

Chapter 3
On the Side

Vegetables & Salads,
Dips, Sauces & Stocks, Preserves

Courgette Boats

MARGARET SIDES, LONGFORD: LIKES READING, COOKING AND WALKING

We used to have courgettes in the garden and my mother gave me this recipe to use up the late summer bounty. We love the combined flavour of the courgette, almonds and cheese. I like to serve it with a mixed grill or as a vegetarian main course with rice.

Serves 8 as a side dish

- 8 small or 4 large courgettes
- 2 tablespoons olive oil
- 1 onion, chopped
- 1 egg, beaten
- ¼ teaspoon mixed dried herbs
- 110g (4oz) ground almonds
- 110g (4oz) grated cheese
- salt and freshly ground black pepper
- 50g (2oz) butter
- 110g (4oz) breadcrumbs (optional)

ICA Tip

The breadcrumbs can be omitted for anyone who is on a gluten-free diet.

1. Preheat oven to 180°C/350°F/Gas 4. Grease and line a baking tray.

2. Halve courgettes lengthway, scoop out seeds and most of the flesh, reserving. Be sure to leave enough skin for the courgette to hold shape once cooked. Chop the reserved flesh, pressing with a spoon to extract juice, and set aside.

3. Place courgette boats hollow-side down onto greased baking tray and roast in preheated oven for about 10 minutes to soften. Remove from oven and set aside to cool.

4. Meanwhile heat a little oil in a heavy frying pan. Add onion and cook gently until softened and translucent. Add chopped courgette flesh and cook for a further five minutes.

5. Allow to cool a little before combining in a mixing bowl with the beaten egg and herbs. Stir in almonds and two thirds of the cheese. Season sparingly (remembering that the cheese will be salty).

6. Turn the boats hollow-side up and spoon the firm mixture into them, but don't overfill. Combine the cheese and breadcrumbs, divide this topping between each courgette and add a knob of butter each. Return to oven for a further 25 minutes, or until bubbling and brown.

Puréed Brussels Sprouts

BRID MALONE, LAOIS: MOTHER OF FIVE, WALKER AND SWIMMER

I like to serve this Brussels sprouts purée at Christmas dinner (see p62). It can be prepared in advance and heated through before serving.

Serves 8
- 450g (1lb) Brussels sprouts
- 150ml (¼ pint) single cream
- 25g (1oz) butter
- 110g (4oz) derinded smoked bacon, chopped
- twist of lemon rind (optional)

1. Trim off the bases of the sprouts and cut a criss-cross on their bottoms with a sharp knife. Add to a saucepan of boiling salted water and simmer until just tender, about five minutes.

2. Drain, return to saucepan over a low heat and toss in a knob butter. Blend with cream and set aside until ready to serve.

3. Reheat gently before serving. Meanwhile lightly fry the smoked bacon in a hot frying pan, drain on kitchen paper and sprinkle over the purée. Finish with a twist of lemon.

Parsnip & Apples

ANNE GABBETT, LIMERICK: DAIRY FARMER'S WIFE AND HOME ECONOMICS TEACHER

*This recipe dates back to the 17th Century and is often served
with roast pork or roast duck.*

Serves 6–8
- 450g (1lb) parsnips, peeled and chopped
- 450g (1lb) apples, peeled and sliced
- 25–50g (1–2oz) butter
- pinch each of ground cinnamon, cloves and nutmeg
- freshly ground pepper, to taste

1. Cover the parsnips in salted water, bring to the boil and cook until soft, about eight minutes.

2. Meanwhile in a separate saucepan, gently cook the apples with a little water until soft. Drain the parsnips and combine with apples, mashing together until smooth.

3. Stir through the butter and spices, season with pepper to taste. Gently heat through before serving.

Lickeen Colcannon

CLAIRE ANN MCDONNELL, WICKLOW: LOVES GARDENING AND THE COUNTRY AIR

This is my original take on traditional colcannon, and was such a winning combination of leftovers that I make it regularly. It's very popular and very tasty.

Makes 6 individual servings
- 675g (1½lb) potatoes, peeled and quartered
- 450g (1lb) green cabbage, shredded
- 50g (2oz) butter
- 1 small onion, finely chopped
- salt and freshly ground black pepper
- 2–3 tablespoons grated Cheddar cheese

to serve
- 6 streaky rashers (optional)

1. Preheat oven to 180°C/350°F/Gas 4.

2. Bring a large pot of salted water to the boil and simmer the potatoes until tender, about 15 minutes. In another pot of boiling water, simmer the shredded cabbage for 10 minutes and drain well.

3. Drain the potatoes once cooked, and mash well with butter. Add the cabbage and onion and season to taste.

4. Divide between six ovenproof ramekin dishes. Lightly score the top of each so it crisps up nicely and sprinkle over grated cheese. Transfer to preheated oven and cook for 20 minutes until it is golden.

5. Meanwhile preheat a grill to hot and cook the streaky rashers until crispy. Cut each in half and serve the individual ramekins garnished with two half slices each.

Puréed Parsnips

BRID MALONE, LAOIS: MOTHER OF FIVE, WALKER AND SWIMMER

This parsnip purée accompanies my roast goose recipe (see p62), but would be a nice simple standby for any roast dinner. It can be prepared in advance and heated through before serving.

Serves 8
- 450g (1lb) parsnips, peeled
- 25g (1oz) butter
- 150ml (¼ pint) single cream
- 2 tablespoons pinenuts

1. Cut the parsnips into even-sized pieces and simmer in salted water until tender, about eight minutes. Drain, return to saucepan over a low heat and toss in a knob butter. Blend with cream and set aside until ready to serve.

2. Toast the pinenuts under the grill or in a dry frying pan, taking care not to burn. Set aside.

3. Reheat purée gently before serving and top with the toasted pinenuts to garnish.

Parisian Potatoes

BRID MALONE, LAOIS: MOTHER OF FIVE, WALKER AND SWIMMER

I like to serve these special potatoes with my Christmas dinner of roast goose (see p62), but they are a nice treat with any roast, especially now that jars of goose fat can be easily bought in most supermarkets.

Serves 8
- 8–16 medium potatoes, scrubbed
- 3–4 tablespoons goose fat
- 1–2 teaspoons salt

1. Preheat oven to 220°C/425°F/Gas 7.

2. Peel the potatoes into round balls, endeavouring to go for as long as possible without breaking the flow in order to produce a smooth surface.

3. Place potato in a large pot of salted water and bring to the boil. Reduce the heat and cook at a gently rolling boil for five minutes. Drain well.

4. Heat a few tablespoons of goose fat in a roasting tray and toss the potatoes in it, making sure they are well coated; if not, add more oil or goose fat. Season generously and roast in preheated oven for 30–40 minutes, or until golden and crispy on the outside and cooked through on the inside.

Coleslaw

AUDREY STARRETT, DONEGAL: JACK OF ALL TRADES

Coleslaw is such a classic salad. It's also extremely simple to make. I tend to make it with white cabbage but red works well too, or you could try half and half.

Serves 6–8 as part of a meal

- 350g (12oz) white or red cabbage, washed and shredded
- 225g (8oz) carrots, peeled and coarsely grated
- 1 spring onion, finely sliced
- 2 tablespoons mayonnaise
- 3 tablespoons plain yoghurt
- salt and freshly ground black pepper
- 1 tablespoon chopped fresh parsley

1. Mix the vegetables well in a large bowl.

2. In a separate bowl combine the yoghurt and the mayonnaise before mixing into the vegetables thoroughly.

3. Season and garnish with chopped parsley to serve.

Granny's Roast Potatoes

GWEN CARTER, WESTMEATH: BELOVED MOTHER AND GRANDMOTHER, RIP

Grannies always make the best roast potatoes: crispy on the outside and soft on the inside. Gwen's family remember her perfect roast potatoes well, and kindly shared the recipe with us to go with her traditional roast chicken (see p65).

Serves 4-6
- 10 large potatoes, peeled and halved
- 3–4 tablespoons olive oil
- salt

ICA Tip
If keeping warm in a low oven for any amount of time, leave uncovered to prevent the potatoes becoming soggy.

1. Preheat the oven to 200°C/400°F/ gas 6.

2. Drop the potatoes into boiling salted water and cook for 10 minutes. Drain off the water and shake the potatoes vigorously in the dry saucepan with the lid on; this roughens the edges of the potatoes so that they will crisp up nicely.

3. Heat a few tablespoons of olive oil in a roasting tray and toss the potatoes in it, making sure they are well coated; add more oil if they aren't. Sprinkle with salt and roast in preheated oven until golden brown and crusty, about 40–50 minutes, occasionally spooning the hot oil over them as they cook.

4. These can be cooked on a lower shelf at the same time as a roast chicken, but you may need to increase the heat towards the end of the cooking to crisp them up nicely.

Spiced Couscous Salad

BREDA MCDONALD, KILKENNY: PASSIONATE BELIEVER IN LOCAL COMMUNITY

This is a versatile salad. I like to serve it with Cajun-spiced fish (see p44) but it also makes a nice addition to a summer barbecue or as a side dish for mixed grills.

Serves 4–6 as a side dish
- 200g (7oz) couscous
- 400ml (¾ pint) boiling water
- 85g (3oz) sultanas
- 1 small courgette, grated
- 1 small carrot, peeled and grated
- 16 cherry tomatoes, halved
- 4 spring onions, chopped
- 85g (3oz) dried apricots, diced
- 50g (2oz) walnuts
- 1 lemon, zest and juice
- ½ teaspoon chilli flakes
- ½ teaspoon ground cumin
- 3 tablespoons oil
- 2 tablespoons chopped fresh mint
- salt and freshly ground black pepper

1. Place the couscous into a large mixing bowl and cover with boiling water. Leave to stand for 10 minutes before fluffing with a fork. Set aside to cool for about 20–30 minutes.

2. Stir through the remaining ingredients and mix well. Season to taste.

HOW TO COOK POTATOES

1. Not all potatoes are created equally. We all have our favourite style of potatoes – experiment with the different varieties available and discover your own.

2. Different styles of potato are suited for different kinds of cooking. Floury potatoes are more traditional in Ireland and are great for everything from baked potatoes to boiled spuds, from chips to mash. Roosters are the most common and versatile floury potato.

3. Waxy potatoes tend to be preferred in classic French cooking. They have a firmer, creamier and moister texture and are suitable for use in salads, for gratins, sautéing, chipping, boiling and roasting, depending on the variety.

4. Store potatoes somewhere cool and dark to prevent them from turning green. Buying potatoes unwashed affords them natural protection from light. Remove potatoes from plastic bags for storage.

5. Potatoes are a good source of Vitamin C. Don't eat potatoes which have turned green, or peel them deeply to remove any of the resulting toxins.

6. If you usually boil potatoes, consider steaming them which is a gentler and healthier method of cooking, as nutrients can leach into the boiling water.

7. If you do boil potatoes, save the starchy, nutrient-rich water drained from boiled potatoes to use to thicken and flavour soups and gravies.

8. When boiling or steaming potatoes to make mashed or roast potatoes, cut into even sized chunks to cook evenly and do not boil too fast or for too long to prevent breaking up the flesh of the potatoes.

9. When making roast potatoes, don't forget to shake the cooked potatoes in the pot to roughen the edges. This will help them crisp up nicely, as does cooking them in goose fat.

10. If keeping roast potatoes warm in the oven for any amount of time, leave them uncovered to prevent them from turning soggy.

Hummus

AN GRIANÁN, LOUTH: ICA ADULT EDUCATION CENTRE

Home-made hummus is so easy to make, especially if you use tinned chickpeas. Tahini is a sesame seed paste traditionally used to give a nutty flavour but if you don't have some handy you may leave it out, or try adding a drop or two of cold-pressed sesame oil instead.

Serves 6–8 as part of a spread of dips

- 400g (14oz) cooked chickpeas
- 2 garlic cloves, crushed
- 3 tablespoons olive oil
- ½ lemon, juice only, or to taste
- 1½ tablespoons tahini (optional)
- salt and freshly ground black pepper

to serve

- toasted pitta bread

1. Drain the chickpeas, reserving some of the liquid from the tin if using, or from the cooking.

2. Blitz the chickpeas, garlic and oil in a blender. Add a couple of tablespoons of lemon juice and salt and pepper to season, and loosen the consistency with some reserved liquid. Pulse to combine well and taste, adding more lemon juice if required.

3. Serve as a dip with toasted pitta bread.

Spinach Dip

STEPHANIE IGOE, LONGFORD: VOLUNTEER AND BUSY MUM OF THREE

I like to serve this as a rustic, chunky dip inside a hollowed-out loaf of bread, but you could opt for a smoother dip made with frozen spinach instead of fresh. It is always very popular at parties.

Serves 8–10 as part of a spread of dips

- 240ml (8fl oz) mayonnaise
- 240ml (8fl oz) sour cream or yoghurt
- 2 spring onions, finely chopped
- 1–2 garlic cloves, finely chopped
- 1–2 tablespoons chopped fresh parsley
- 1 packet dried vegetable soup mix
- 450g frozen spinach (or 250g fresh spinach)

to serve

- vegetable crudités (carrots, cucumber, celery, courgette or radishes)
- 1 round pumpernickel loaf or white bloomer (optional)

1. Combine the mayonnaise and sour cream or yoghurt, stir in the spring onion, garlic, parsley and powdered soup. Chill for a couple of hours. Meanwhile allow the frozen spinach to defrost, if using.

2. Drain the defrosted spinach, if using, and finely chop. Alternatively, for a more rustic dip, roughly chop the fresh spinach. Fold into the chilled dip and mix well.

3. Hollow out inside of loaf, if using, and tear the inner bread into chunks for dipping. Prepare your vegetables of choice, cutting into thin batons. Serve dip inside the hollowed bread or simply in a serving bowl, with bread chunks and vegetables for dipping.

Fresh Tomato Salsa

AN GRIANÁN, LOUTH: ICA ADULT EDUCATION CENTRE

This fresh salsa is very quick to make up.

*Serves 8–10 as part of a
spread of dips*

- 6 large ripe tomatoes
- 2–4 garlic cloves, finely chopped
- 1 red onion, finely diced
- 1 green pepper, cored and finely diced
- 1 green chilli, deseeded and finely diced (optional)
- 1 bunch of fresh coriander, roughly chopped
- 4 tablespoons olive oil, or to taste
- pinch of salt, or to taste

to serve
- tortilla chips

1. If you want to peel the tomatoes, cut a cross in the top of each and place them a few at a time in a large bowl. Cover in boiling water and leave to sit for about a minute, during which time the skin will tighten and begin to peel back. Remove from the water, peel and set aside. Repeat with the remaining tomatoes.

2. Chop the tomatoes fairly chunkily and mix with the remaining ingredients, adding enough oil to bind and seasoning with salt to taste. Chill and serve with tortilla chips.

Salsa Roja

STEPHANIE IGOE, LONGFORD: VOLUNTEER AND BUSY MUM OF THREE

This rich, cooked tomato salsa makes a great alternative to jars of commercial salsa, and will keep very well once cooked. Based on tinned tomatoes, it's a good option when fresh tomatoes are out of season.

Serves 10–12 as part of a spread of dip

- 4 tablespoons oil
- 1 red onion, chopped finely
- 2 tablespoons chilli powder
- 1½ tablespoons dried oregano
- 1 teaspoon salt
- 800g (28oz) tinned chopped tomatoes
- 1 green pepper, cored and finely chopped
- 1 red pepper, cored and finely chopped

to serve
- tortilla chips

1. Heat the oil in a large heavy-based saucepan and cook onion over a gentle heat until soft and translucent.

2. Add all the remaining ingredients bar the peppers. Stir in the spices, herbs and salt and cook for a minute or two to release the aromas before adding the tomatoes. Bring to a gentle boil and simmer for 25 minutes.

3. Add peppers, cook for a further 10 minutes and remove from heat to cool completely. Serve with tortilla chips.

Sweet Chilli Sauce

KAY MCGUIRL, WICKLOW: LOVES TO SWIM AND WALK THE MINI-MARATHON

This will keep in the fridge for up to a week and makes a handy condiment for grills and barbecues. You can deseed the chillies for a milder sauce but you want a little fire to stand up to the sweetness.

Makes about 500ml
- 2 red chillies, trimmed
- 2 garlic cloves, peeled
- 200ml (7fl oz) rice wine vinegar
- 260ml (9fl oz) water
- 250g (9oz) sugar
- 6 teaspoons cornflour
- salt and freshly ground black pepper

1. Combine the chilli, garlic and vinegar in a food processor and blend until smooth. In a large saucepan heat the sugar and water until simmering and then add the chilli mixture.

2. In a small bowl, combine the cornflour with a little water and mix to a smooth paste. Whisk into the simmering pot and continue to stir over a medium heat until smooth.

3. Remove from the heat and allow to cool before seasoning to taste.

Basil Pesto

MARY O'NEILL, WICKLOW: RETIRED TEACHER WITH A GRÁ FOR TRAVEL

I was introduced to pesto by my children. My own mum or grandmother would never have heard of it. Now we use it so often – over pasta, on bread, on toast, even by the spoonful. My version has the additional treat of Brazil nuts.

Makes about 500ml

- 125g (4½oz) fresh basil, roughly chopped
- 230ml (8fl oz) extra virgin olive oil
- 65g (2½oz) pinenuts
- 25g (1oz) Brazil nuts, roughly chopped (optional)
- 65g (2½oz) Parmesan cheese, grated
- 2 garlic cloves, minced

ICA Tip

Covering pesto with a slick of oil and chilling will help to keep it fresh.

1. Place the basil in a blender. Pour in a tablespoon of the oil and blend to a paste.

2. Gradually add pinenuts, Brazil nuts (if using), Parmesan cheese, garlic and remaining oil. Continue to blend until smooth.

Damson & Apple Sauce

BRID MALONE, LAOIS: MOTHER OF FIVE, WALKER AND SWIMMER

This home-made damson sauce is to accompany the roast goose recipe (see p62) but would work well with other poultry roasts or game birds such as pheasant.

Serves 8

- 225g (8oz) damsons (fresh or frozen)
- 250ml (½ pint) cider
- 1 tablespoon goose fat or oil
- ½ medium onion, chopped
- 225g (8oz) cooking apples, peeled and chopped
- 2 pinches ground cloves
- 2 pinches ground mace
- 2 tablespoons caster sugar

1. Soak the damsons overnight in cider to plump up.

2. To make the sauce, heat the damsons and cider in a small saucepan and simmer until soft. Strain the fruit, reserving the cider, and chop into small pieces.

3. In a frying pan, sauté the onion in a little goose fat or oil until it begins to soften. Add chopped apples and simmer until soft and fluffy.

4. Stir in damsons, caster sugar and spices. Taste and adjust with sugar or spices as necessary. Reheat gently before serving.

Goose Giblet Stock

BRID MALONE, LAOIS: MOTHER OF FIVE, WALKER AND SWIMMER

This quick stock uses up the remaining giblets from the roast goose recipe (see p62) and gives a great depth of flavour to the final gravy. Giblets are the edible offal of poultry, usually including the heart, gizzards and liver and sometimes the neck of the bird.

Makes about 400ml
- goose giblets
- 570ml (1 pint) water
- 1 onion, halved
- 1 bay leaf
- salt and freshly ground black pepper

1. In a stockpot, simmer the giblets for about an hour in water together with the onion, bay leaf and a little seasoning.

2. Chill or freeze until ready to use.

Chicken Stock

GWEN CARTER, WESTMEATH: BELOVED MOTHER AND GRANDMOTHER, RIP

It really is worth getting into the habit of making your own chicken stock. You'll be glad of it the next time you want to make a home-made gravy for your Sunday roast, or give a boost of flavour to soup.

Makes about 1 litre
- 1 onion, halved
- 1 bay leaf
- 1 chicken carcass
- 2 litres (4 pints) cold water
- salt and freshly ground black pepper

1. Place the onion and bay leaf in a large stockpot, add the chicken carcass and cover with cold water. Bring to the boil, then reduce the heat and simmer gently for two hours.

2. Strain, check the seasoning and allow to cool. Refrigerate for a couple of hours and skim any fat from the surface of the stock. Use within three days or freeze in small containers for ease of use.

HOW TO MAKE PRESERVES

1. Home-made preserves such as jams, marmalades and chutneys are a great way to use up a seasonal glut of a particular ingredient. There was a time when many ICA members grew their own garden produce, a practice coming back into popularity in recent years.

2. Making your own preserves can be a great way to save or even earn money – whether saving on Christmas gifts, swapping with friends and neighbours or even selling in your local market as ICA women have done for many years.

3. Remember that quality begets quality. Excellent fruit and vegetables will give better results than bruised or tired produce. Fresh spices make a difference too. Slightly underripe fruit will produce higher pectin levels than ripe fruit, allowing jams to set better.

4. It is important to dissolve sugar fully before boiling rapidly for a good five minutes, or as long as the recipe indicates. Preheating sugar in a low oven helps to speed up the cooking process.

5. To test if jam is at setting point, place a plate in the freezer box of the fridge for five or ten minutes. Pop a spoonful of jam on the plate. If the jam wrinkles when pressed, it is ready to bottle. If not set, continue boiling for a little longer and test again. Alternatively use a jam thermometer to check for setting temperature of 105°C (220°F).

6. Correctly sterilised jars are crucial. Wash jars well in hot soapy water, rinse thoroughly and place still slightly wet in a cool oven for 30 minutes or in a microwave on full heat for 60 seconds. Alternatively, boil top-down in a large pot of boiling water for five minutes.

7. Always add hot jam to hot jars, never hot jam to cold jars or cold jam to hot jars.

8. Seal home-made preserves with a piece of parchment tied with twine or secured with rubber bands, or alternatively look out for packets of jam covers in the supermarket.

9. Always label preserves clearly, and include the month of production.

10. If home-made jam crystallises you can reboil to break up the crystals although this can produce a burnt flavour. Alternatively, use it as a sweetener when stewing fruit like rhubarb for tarts or crumbles.

Redcurrant & Orange Jam

KATHLEEN GORMAN, LAOIS: BAKER, KNITTER AND KEEN READER

A beautiful bitter-sweet breakfast jam, this is wonderful spread on freshly baked brown soda bread.

Makes about 6 jars
- 900g (2lb) redcurrants, stalks removed
- 2 oranges, finely sliced
- 900g (2lb) granulated sugar

1. Preheat oven to 140°C/275°F/Gas 1.

2. Combine the redcurrants and orange slices in a saucepan over a gentle heat to release their juices. Bring slowly to the boil and cook gently for 10 minutes.

3. Meanwhile, warm the sugar for a few minutes in the low oven. Add the warmed sugar to the simmering fruit and bring slowly back to the boil. Boil rapidly for seven to ten minutes or until setting point is reached. (See p113 for how to test setting point.)

4. Remove from the heat and let the pan stand for 15 minutes. Spoon into sterilised jars (see p113), seal well and label.

Blackberry & Apple Jam

ANNE MARIA DENNISON, LIMERICK: FORMER ICA NATIONAL PRESIDENT

This is a lovely jam to make use of an autumnal glut of berries and apples.

Makes about 8–10 jars
- 1kg (2lb) blackberries
- 500g (1lb) cooking apples
- 150ml (¼ pint) water
- 1½kg (3lb) sugar
- 2 lemons, juice only

1. In a large heavy-based pot, simmer the blackberries in half the water over a gentle heat until soft, stirring to prevent sticking. In a separate saucepan, stew the apples in the remaining water until soft and add to the blackberries.

2. Add the sugar and lemon juice, stirring continuously until the sugar has been dissolved. Increase the heat and boil rapidly, stirring for 10–15 minutes.

3. To test if jam is at setting point, place a plate in the freezer box of the fridge for five or ten minutes. Pop a spoonful of jam on the plate and return to the fridge or freezer to cool for a few minutes. If the jam wrinkles when pressed, it is ready to bottle. If not set, continue boiling for a little longer and test again.

4. Leave to cool a little and pour into warm sterilised jars (see p113). Seal well and label.

All Season Fruity Jam

JOAN HATTON, WICKLOW: LOVES WORKING WITH MOTHER NATURE

For many years I made preserves for the local Country Market from my home-grown produce. One evening I decided to experiment with what was in my fruit bowl. It turned into this wonderful jam, now a hot favourite amongst my family. You can add a mix of whatever fruit is in season and it keeps very well.

Makes about 6–8 jars
- 6 Granny Smith apples, washed
- 6 red apples, washed
- 2 oranges, washed
- 1 lemon, washed
- 2 teaspoons cloves
- 1 teaspoon cinnamon
- 4 bananas, peeled and roughly chopped
- 1kg (2.2lb) sugar

ICA Tip
This jam makes a great standby dessert poured over ice-cream or spread into a sponge roll.

1. Core the unpeeled apples, chop into small pieces and place in a large saucepan. Squeeze over the juice of oranges and lemon. Stir in cloves and cinnamon together with a couple of mugs of water.

2. Chop the peel and pulp of the squeezed orange and lemon into small pieces, add to the pot and cook over a medium heat at a gentle simmer for about 20 minutes, or until the fruit peel softens.

3. Remove from heat and add chopped bananas. Add sugar, stirring until fully dissolved. Return to a low heat and slowly bring to boil, stirring to prevent sticking, and then boil rapidly for four to five minutes.

4. To sterilise the jars, wash them well and place them still slightly wet in a microwave and give them a quick blast on full heat for 60 seconds.

5. Remove jam from heat and pour directly into sterilised jars. Seal with a piece of parchment, cover and label.

Three Fruit Marmalade

MAUREEN QUIGLEY, WICKLOW: LOVES TO READ AND BAKE

This is a really simple recipe that I created using readily available ingredients. I like it because most of the cooking needs no attention.

Makes about 6 jars
- 2 lemons, scrubbed
- 1 orange, scrubbed
- 1 grapefruit, scrubbed
- 850ml (1½ pints) water
- 1½kg (3lb) sugar (approximately)

You will need
- slow cooker or crock pot
- muslin and string

ICA Tip
> It is essential to transfer the fruit to a heavy saucepan in order to reach the full rolling boil required for good marmalade and jam making.

1. Slice lemons and orange finely and place in a large mixing bowl, removing and reserving pips as you go. Peel the rind from grapefruit with vegetable peeler. Slice very fine and add to the mixing bowl. Peel pith from grapefruit, finely chop and reserve. Finely slice the remaining grapefruit flesh and add to the mixing bowl.

2. Combine the reserved pith and pips in a muslin bag, tied with a piece of string. Place fruit and muslin bag into slow cooker, pour over water, cover with lid and cook on low setting for 8–10 hours or overnight.

3. Preheat oven to 140°C/275°F/Gas 1.

4. Allow to cool and remove muslin bag. Transfer the pulp into a clean heavy-based saucepan with a cup, keeping count of how many cups as you go. Measure an equal quantity of cups of sugar into a baking tray, and warm in preheated oven for about five minutes.

5. Add warmed sugar to the pulp, stirring until dissolved. Bring to a rolling boil and cook rapidly for about 15–20 minutes, until setting point is reached (see p113). Remove from heat and cool for about 15 minutes to allow the peel to distribute evenly through the marmalade. Ladle into warm sterilised jars (see p113). Cover, seal well and label.

Courgette Jam

MAUREEN QUIGLEY, WICKLOW: LOVES TO READ AND BAKE

This unique jam makes a fine accompaniment to any bread or scone, and is a great way to make use of a seasonal bounty. For me, this kind of recipe is the epitome of home-cooking: using home-grown produce to create something you would not come across on any supermarket shelf.

Makes about 10–12 jars
- 2.8kg (6lb) courgette or marrow
- 2.8kg (6lb) sugar (approximately)
- 1 teaspoon vegetable oil
- 1 teaspoon preserved ginger, finely chopped
- 6 lemons, juice only

1. Peel the courgette or marrow, scoop out the seeds and cut flesh into thin chunks. Weigh this flesh and transfer to a stainless-steel or plastic bowl. Weigh an equal amount of sugar and add to bowl, mixing well. Cover and leave somewhere cool to steep for a day or two, stirring occasionally.

2. Transfer to a large saucepan greased very lightly with a little oil. Add ginger and lemon juice, bring to the boil and boil for about 30 minutes, stirring occasionally.

3. With a jam thermometer, check if jam has reached setting point of 105°C/220°F (or see p113 for alternative setting tests).

4. Pour carefully into hot sterilised jars (see p113). Cover immediately, seal well and label.

Tomato & Apple Chutney

ANNE MARIA DENNISON, LIMERICK: FORMER ICA NATIONAL PRESIDENT

This recipe works as well with unripe green tomatoes as it does with ripe red ones. The longer you leave it to mature and mellow, the better it will taste.

Makes about 6 jars
- 1.5kg (3lb) tomatoes, cored and chopped
- 3 large cooking apples, cored and chopped
- 3 large onions, chopped
- 150g (5½oz) sultanas or raisins
- 2 garlic cloves, chopped (optional)
- 2 heaped teaspoons mustard powder
- 1½ teaspoons ground ginger
- 1½ teaspoons cayenne pepper
- 1 teaspoon salt
- 600ml (1 pint) vinegar
- 350g (12oz) brown sugar

1. In a large saucepan, combine all ingredients except the sugar. Bring to the boil and reduce heat. Simmer uncovered for about 90 minutes or until all fruits are soft, stirring occasionally to prevent sticking.

2. Add the sugar and simmer for another 30 minutes or so. It is ready for bottling when a wooden spoon drawn through the mix leaves a track.

3. Purée in a liquidiser and transfer to sterilised jars (see p113). Seal well, label and store somewhere cool and dark for at least three months to mature.

Apple & Ginger Chutney

ANNA SINNOTT, WICKLOW: BUSY HOUSEWIFE WHO LOVES TO BAKE

This is a recipe that my mother used to make and is still a firm family favourite. It pairs well with cheese and cold meats, and is a nice addition to a picnic.

Makes about 8–10 jars
- 2.8kg (6lb) apples
- 900g (2lb) sultanas
- 350g (12oz) preserved ginger
- 1½ litres (3 pints) vinegar
- 1½kg (3½lb) sugar
- 1½ teaspoons salt
- 1 teaspoon allspice

1. Peel, core and chop the apples into small pieces. Roughly chop sultanas and ginger.

2. Combine the vinegar, sugar, salt and allspice in a large saucepan and bring to the boil. Add apples and simmer for 10 minutes before adding sultanas and ginger.

3. Simmer until the mixture thickens. Pour into sterilised jars (see p113), seal well and cover.

Beetroot Chutney

ANNA SINNOTT, WICKLOW: BUSY HOUSEWIFE WHO LOVES TO BAKE

This is another recipe that my mother used to make and its unusual flavours make it a favourite of mine. I use a ready-bought pickling spice mix when I have it or make my own with coriander seeds, mustard seeds, allspice, ground ginger, black peppercorns and a couple of bay leaves.

Makes about 5–6 jars
- 1¼kg (3lb) beetroot
- 450g (1lb) apples
- 450g (1lb) onions, chopped
- 570ml (1 pint) spiced white vinegar (or white wine vinegar)
- 25g (1oz) pickling spice
- 450g (1lb) white sugar
- 2 teaspoons salt

You will need
- muslin and string

1. To cook the beetroot, scrub gently but thoroughly, toss in oil and roast in a medium oven for 30–60 minutes or until tender. Allow to cool, peel and finely dice. Peel, core and chop the apples.

2. In a large heavy-based saucepan, cover the onions in a little vinegar and simmer over a gentle heat for about five minutes or until they begin to soften and turn translucent.

3. Add the beetroot and apples. Tie the spices securely in a muslin bag and add to the pot. Cook gently until fruit is soft, stirring from time to time.

4. Add remaining vinegar along with the sugar and salt, stirring thoroughly. Increase the heat and cook at a steady boil until thick.

5. Remove pickling spices and pour chutney into hot sterilised jars (see p113). Seal well and ideally mature for a week or two before using to allow the flavours to develop.

Chapter 4
Baking & Sweet Things

Breads, Scones & Pastry, Cakes,
Tarts & Sweet Snacks, Puddings & Desserts

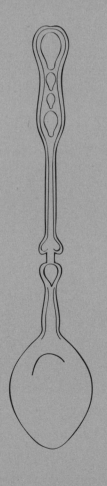

Bacon & Thyme Scones

EDWARD HAYDEN, KILKENNY: TV CHEF AND FOOD WRITER

I love the combination of flavours in these particular scones. They are ideal for light snacks, lunch box fillers or as an individual bread option at a dinner party.

Makes 10–12
- 140g (5oz) bacon lardons
- 450g (1lb) plain flour
- 1 heaped teaspoon baking powder
- ½ teaspoon cayenne pepper or paprika
- pinch of salt
- 85g (3oz) cold butter, diced
- 85g (3oz) grated cheddar cheese, plus extra for topping if desired
- 2 teaspoons chopped fresh thyme
- 2 large eggs
- 200ml (7fl oz) buttermilk
- 3 tablespoons milk
- 1–2 handfuls pumpkin seeds

You will need
- baking tray or sheet

1. Heat a heavy pan and dry fry the bacon lardons until they are beginning to brown up. There is no need to cook until crispy as they will be going into the oven. Set aside to cool.

2. Preheat the oven to 180°C/350°F/Gas 4. Grease a flat baking tray or sheet.

3. Sieve the flour, baking powder and cayenne pepper into a large mixing bowl. Add the salt and diced butter. Gently rub the butter into the flour until it resembles fine breadcrumbs. Add the grated cheese, cooked bacon and chopped thyme.

4. In a separate bowl lightly whisk one large egg. Make a well in the dry ingredients and add the whisked egg, mixing with a knife to integrate. Gradually mix in enough buttermilk to achieve a soft sticky dough.

5. Roll out on a lightly floured surface and cut into 10–12 equal-sized shapes using either a sharp knife or a scone cutter.

6. Brush the scones with the remaining egg beaten with a little milk, and sprinkle with the pumpkins seeds or a little extra cheese if you wish. Bake on baking tray in preheated oven for 25 minutes or until golden brown. Best served warm with butter.

Potato Scones

AN GRIANÁN, LOUTH: ICA ADULT EDUCATION CENTRE

This is another favourite amongst An Grianán staff, many of whom make it at home as a great way to use up leftover mashed potatoes. Lovely with soup for lunch, or reheat them in a pan to serve with a breakfast fry of sausages and rashers.

Makes 8
- 225g (8oz) cooked mashed potato
- 225g (8oz) self-raising flour
- 2 teaspoons baking powder
- ½ teaspoon salt
- 85g (3oz) butter, at room temperature
- 1 teaspoon mixed dried herbs
- 125ml (4fl oz) milk

to finish
- 1 egg, beaten (optional)

You will need
- 21cm (8in) cake tin
- baking tray

1. Preheat oven to 200°C/400°F/Gas 6. Place a baking tray or sheet into the oven. Grease a 21cm (8in) cake tin.

2. Place the mashed potato in a large mixing bowl. In a separate bowl, sieve the flour and baking powder. Rub in the butter until it resembles breadcrumbs and mix in the herbs. Add to the mashed potato and work the two mixtures together, gradually adding just enough milk to bind – you may not need it all, depending on how dry the potatoes are.

3. Turn the dough onto a lightly floured surface and knead very lightly until pliable. Roll into a ball, flatten and roll out to a circle of about 21cm (8in) diameter. Transfer to prepared cake tin. Cut into eight wedges and transfer tin to preheated baking tray.

4. Brush with beaten egg to glaze, if desired. Bake for 25 minutes in preheated oven until well-risen and golden brown. Best eaten hot with lots of butter.

ICA Tip
If you wish to make potato bread instead, simply roll the dough out thinner and cook on a dry non-stick pan until golden brown on each side.

Pizza Muffins

AN GRIANÁN, LOUTH: ICA ADULT EDUCATION CENTRE

This is a great recipe for lunch boxes or for a family picnic in the summer. Use chopped cherry tomatoes if you have no sun-dried ones, and feel free to add any leftover meat like chicken, ham or chorizo for extra flavour.

Makes 9–12
- 450g (1lb) plain flour
- 2 teaspoons baking powder
- pinch of salt
- 50g (2oz) cold butter, coarsely chopped
- 140g (5oz) strong cheese (Wensleydale or farmhouse cheddar)
- 110g (4oz) bacon, diced and cooked
- 50g (2oz) sun-dried tomatoes, chopped
- 2 tablespoons parsley chopped
- salt and freshly ground black pepper
- 2 eggs
- 1 tablespoon olive oil
- 400ml (¾ pint) milk

You will need
- 12-cup muffin tin

1. Preheat oven to 200°C/400°F/Gas 6. Lightly grease muffin tin and dust with flour.

2. Sieve the flour, baking powder and salt into a large bowl. Add the chopped butter but do not rub in. Roughly grate the cheese and add with the bacon, tomatoes and parsley. Season and mix well.

3. Beat the eggs, oil and milk together. Make a well in the centre of the flour mixture and and gently fold the liquid in to form a soft dough, taking care not to overmix.

4. Divide the mixture into between 12 muffin cups and bake in preheated oven for 15–20 minutes, or until golden brown.

Sweet Fruit Scones

KATHLEEN GORMAN, LAOIS: BAKER, KNITTER AND KEEN READER

I love to bake and when I make scones I like to make a big family-sized batch, especially if any of my nine grandchildren are around. These sweet scones are a perfect excuse to enjoy some afternoon tea, complete with home-made jam and whipped cream for a real grown-up treat for all ages.

Makes about 18
- 600g (1lb 5oz) plain flour
- 2 teaspoons bicarbonate of soda
- ½ teaspoon salt
- 125g (4½oz) cold butter
- 110g (4oz) caster sugar
- 110g (4oz) sultanas
- 50g (2oz) mixed peel
- 3 eggs
- 265ml (9fl oz) milk

to serve
- home-made jam
- whipped cream

You will need
- baking tray or sheet

1. Preheat oven to 180°C/350°F/Gas 4. Place a baking tray or sheet into the oven.

2. Sieve flour, soda and salt into a large mixing bowl. Cut butter into pieces and rub into flour until it resembles breadcrumbs. Add sugar, sultanas and peel.

3. In a small bowl, beat two of the eggs and add the milk. Make a well in the dry ingredients and pour in most of the liquid. Mix to a consistency moist enough to knead without being sticky, adding more liquid if required (you may not need all of it).

4. Turn onto a lightly floured surface and knead lightly to form a smooth dough. Roll out the dough with a lightly floured rolling pin to a thickness of about 2cm (¾in) thick. Cut out scones into desired shape, using a knife for square scones or a cutter for round ones.

5. Brush with the remaining beaten egg and bake on a lightly floured, preheated baking tray for 15–20 minutes or until golden brown. Serve warm with home-made jam and whipped cream.

Walnut & Treacle Bread

EDWARD HAYDEN, KILKENNY: TV CHEF AND FOOD WRITER

*Our home is rarely without a loaf of this delicious bread. I like to include walnuts
and treacle but feel free to leave them out if you wish.
The mixture can also be spooned into muffin tins and baked for
25 minutes at 180°C/350°F/Gas 4.*

Makes 900g (2lb) loaf
- 350g (12oz) coarse wholemeal flour
- 2oz (50g) plain flour
- 2oz (50g) porridge oats
- pinch of salt
- 2 teaspoons bicarbonate of soda
- 2 large eggs
- 1 dessertspoon sunflower oil
- 2 tablespoons dark treacle
- 480ml (1 pint) buttermilk
- 50g (2oz) walnut halves, roughly crushed

You will need
- 900g (2lb) loaf tin

ICA Tip
If you don't have
buttermilk you could sour
some fresh milk with a
little lemon juice or natural
yoghurt, stirring in and
leaving to rest for a few
minutes.

1. Preheat oven to 170°C/325°F/Gas 3. Grease the loaf tin.

2. Combine three quarters of the porridge oats with both flours in a large mixing bowl, add the salt, sieve in the soda and mix well.

3. In a separate bowl beat the eggs together with the oil and treacle and add to the dry mixture. Pour in the buttermilk, add the walnuts and mix to a fairly loose, sloppy consistency.

4. Pour into greased tin, smoothing the top with a wet spoon. Sprinkle over the remaining oats and bake in the preheated oven for one hour. Remove bread from tin and return to the oven for a further 20 minutes.

5. Allow to cool on a wire rack before slicing. This bread stays fresh for about four or five days and freezes well.

Brown Soda Bread

CONNIE MCEVOY, LOUTH: RETIRED FARMER AND CRAFT EXPERT

As the eldest of ten, from the age of 12 I would make several cakes of this wheaten bread every Saturday based on my grandmother's recipe. We always mixed it by hand and I still measure it by hand, using four large fistfuls of wholemeal flour and two smaller fistfuls of plain flour.

Makes 1 loaf
- 175g (6oz) plain flour
- 1 teaspoon salt
- 1½ heaped teaspoons bicarbonate of soda
- 450g (1lb) wholemeal flour, plus a little extra for dusting
- 1 egg
- 400ml (¾ pint) buttermilk

You will need
- 20cm (8in) round cake tin or Swissroll tin

ICA Tip
Cooling on a wire rack will produce a good crust. If a soft crust is preferred, cool the bread wrapped in a clean tea cloth.

1. Preheat oven to 220°C/425°F/Gas 7. Dust selected tin generously with flour (we always used a Swiss roll tin for this bread).

2. Sieve the plain flour, salt and soda into a large mixing bowl. Add the wholemeal flour and mix well, lifting the dry ingredients just above the bowl's rim in order to circulate air and produce a lighter bread.

3. Beat the egg in a small bowl and beat in the buttermilk. Make a well in the dry ingredients, add the liquid and mix to a soft dough with a wooden spoon or by hand.

4. Bring dough together with flour-dusted fingers and turn out on a lightly floured surface. Knead lightly into the smooth desired shape. If the dough is sticky, dust over a little more flour and knead it in to make it more manageable. Transfer to prepared tin, dust with wholemeal and cut a cross on top with a sharp knife to allow to rise evenly.

5. Bake in preheated oven for 30–40 minutes. Remove from tin and tap the base of the bread. If it sounds hollow it us cooked, if not return to the oven for a few more minutes. Cool on a wire rack before serving with country butter and home-made jam for the full experience.

Rough Puff Pastry

MARIE MCGUIRK, LOUTH: COOKERY TUTOR AND ASPIRING GOLFER

This rough puff pastry recipe makes a pastry lid for the Rabbit Pie (see p63) but would also work well with the Pork and Cider Stroganoff (p70), and is a handy one to have in your repertoire.

Makes 500g
- 250g (10oz) strong flour, plus a little extra
- 1 teaspoon salt
- 250g (10oz) butter, at room temperature
- 150ml (¼ pint) cold water

ICA Tip
Pastry freezes well, for up to three months if well wrapped. Defrost for a couple of hours and allow to return to room temperature before using.

1. Sieve the flour and salt into a bowl. Cut the butter into quarters. Rub one quarter into the flour until it resembles fine breadcrumbs. Cut the remaining butter into walnut-sized pieces and toss these in the flour. Gradually add just enough water to bind and form a soft elastic dough, but take care do not make it too wet.

2. Sprinkle some extra flour onto a clean, broad surface and turn the dough out onto the flour. Knead very lightly until smooth and then roll away from you into a long rectangle, keeping the edges straight as you roll. Mark the dough widthways into three even pieces. Fold the top third down over the middle third, and then fold the bottom third up over these two.

3. Turn the pastry round clockwise so that the folds are facing towards your right hand and repeat this rolling and folding process. Wrap the pastry in clingfilm and chill for 20 minutes.

4. Unwrap and place with the fold again facing your right hand. Repeat the rolling and folding process for a third time. Wrap well and store in the fridge until ready to use.

HOW TO GET BAKING

1. Baking is so easy but it can be intimidating. If you're new to it, try starting with scones and biscuits to build your confidence before moving on to small cakes.

2. There's an old song of yesteryear that sang "If I knew you were coming I'd have baked a cake". But why wait until someone comes? Bake a cake and have it ready to serve. A simple fruit cake keeps very well.

3. Stock up on baking parchment for lining tins and trays and clingfilm for wrapping pastry. Try keeping your clingfilm in the fridge: it will never stick to itself and be easy to unroll.

4. Handle pastry as little and lightly as possible, kneading only as much as necessary. On the other hand, pastry freezes well – up to three months if well-sealed. Allow to come fully back to room temperature before using.

5. Keep a small jar of dry beans for baking pastry blind. These beans are placed on a sheet of parchment while par-baking pastry shells for quiches, tarts and flans. They weigh down the pastry to prevent it rising, and can be re-used.

6. Get organised before you get baking, with all ingredients weighed out and prepared, tins lined and oven preheated at correct temperature. A metal skewer is worth having to hand to test if breads or cakes are cooked.

7. Get to know your oven and adjust temperatures and timings accordingly. Most ovens deliver slightly different temperatures. If yours is a fan oven, you'll need to opt for slightly lower temperatures than those given (eg 180°C instead of 200°C).

8. Baking is as much a science as an art. Pay close attention to recipes: if they call for one teaspoon, use one level teaspoon – if they mean heaped they'll say it!

9. Use a weighing scales and consider investing in a set of measuring spoons. The difference between a tablespoon and a dessertspoon can make all the difference in your results.

10. Use butter in baking where possible. It gives great results, is as cheap as margarine and many now believe it is much better for your health. Irish butter is the best in the world, thanks to all our green green grass.

Upside-Down Pear Cake

AN GRIANÁN, LOUTH: ICA ADULT EDUCATION CENTRE

This old-fashioned upside-down cake is as easy as they get and very versatile too, working a treat with many fresh and tinned fruits. It's delicious hot or cold, and the fruit will keep the sponge nicely moist for several days.

Serves 6
- 50g (2oz) butter, melted
- 25g (1oz) caster sugar
- 25g (1oz) light brown sugar
- 2–3 ripe pears

for the sponge batter
- 100g (4oz) softened butter or margarine
- 100g (4oz) caster sugar
- 100g (4oz) plain flour
- 2 teaspoons baking powder
- ½ teaspoon ground cinnamon
- ¼ teaspoon mixed spice
- 2 eggs

to serve
- whipped cream

You will need
- 23cm (9in) round or square cake tin, or smaller individual cake tins

1. Preheat oven to 180°C/350°F/Gas 4. Grease 23cm (9in) cake tin with a little of the melted butter. Alternatively, you could make four individual cakes in mini-tins if desired.

2. Mix caster and brown sugars into the remaining melted butter and pour into prepped tin. Peel, halve and core the pears and arrange curved-side down in the butter and sugar mixture.

3. To make the sponge batter, combine all the ingredients in a large mixing bowl and mix thoroughly for one minute. Pour this over the pears and bake in preheated oven for 40 minutes, or until firm to the touch.

4. Remove from the oven and cool for at least ten minutes before loosening the cake from the sides of the tin and inverting onto a rimmed plate. Spoon any remaining juices onto the cake.

5. Slice into individual portions and serve warm with whipped cream. The leftovers are delicious served cold as a cake for afternoon tea.

ICA Tip
You can vary the fruits according to the season – maybe apple and blackberry in autumn, or pineapple in winter.

Light Lemon Sponge

CAROLINE POWER, MEATH: LOVER OF CRAFTS AND READING

I have been cooking this tried and trusted recipe since my teen years when I learnt it in home economics class. It since became my signature dish for family gatherings. It is a very easy cake but one that can be dressed up or down by varying the filling.

Serves 8
- 50g (2oz) plain flour
- 50g (2oz) cornflour
- 1 teaspoon baking powder
- pinch of salt
- 4 eggs, separated
- 110g (4oz) caster sugar

for the lemon filling
- 75g (3oz) butter
- 150g (6oz) icing sugar, sieved
- 1 lemon, finely grated zest and juice

You will need
- 2 x 20cm (8in) sandwich tins

ICA Tip
This works very well with fresh or tinned fruit, either as a filling or served as a fruit salad on the side.

1. Preheat oven to 200°C/400°F/Gas 6. Grease sandwich tins.

2. Sieve the flour, cornflour, baking powder and salt together.

3. In a separate large mixing bowl, beat egg whites into stiff peaks. Gradually add caster sugar as you continue to whisk until thick and smooth. Finally whisk in egg yolks.

4. Quickly and lightly fold in sieved ingredients with a metal spoon and divide mixture between prepared tins. Bake in preheated oven for 15 minutes or until an inserted skewer comes out clean.

5. Meanwhile to make the lemon filling, cream together butter and sugar until light and fluffy. Beat in lemon zest and one dessertspoon of lemon juice.

6. Once cooked, allow to cool a little before removing from tins. Set on a wire rack to cool completely and then sandwich together with flavoured filling.

Grandma's Rhubarb Tart

PATRICIA ACHESON, CAVAN: FARMER AND COMMUNITY WORKER

This very traditional style of tart brings me back to visiting my grandma on the homefarm and how we longed for a second helping. When no-one was looking we made do with licking the plate. A really basic recipe, it resembles white soda bread with a deep fruit filling.

Serves 8
- 340g (12oz) plain flour
- 85g (3oz) margarine
- 275g (10oz) caster sugar
- ½ teaspoon bicarbonate of soda
- pinch of salt
- 1 egg
- 180ml (6fl oz) buttermilk or sour milk
- 675g (1½lb) rhubarb, finely chopped

to finish
- 1 egg
- pinch of salt
- 1 tablespoon caster sugar

to serve
- ice-cream, cream or hot runny custard

You will need
- 25cm (10in) round pyrex pie dish

1. Preheat oven to 180°C/350°F/Gas 4.

2. Sieve flour into large mixing bowl and rub in margarine until it resembles fine breadcrumbs. Mix in 50g (2oz) sugar, soda and a pinch of salt and make a well in the centre. Beat an egg and mix with buttermilk. Add this liquid to dry ingredients, folding in and mixing well until it forms a soft dough.

3. Turn dough onto a lightly floured surface and roll into a round. Divide mixture into two halves and gently roll out one half large enough to cover base of pyrex pie dish. Transfer to dish.

4. Beat the remaining egg with a pinch of salt and dampen edges of dough with a little of this egg wash. Add rhubarb and sprinkle with remaining sugar. Roll out the remaining dough and cover the rhubarb, pressing edges together to seal.

5. Pierce a hole in the centre for the steam to escape. Brush with remaining egg wash and sprinkle with caster sugar. Bake in preheated oven for 45–60 minutes. Allow to cool slightly before serving with ice-cream, cream or custard.

Apple Tart

LIZ WALL, WICKLOW: BUSY MUM AND ICA NATIONAL PRESIDENT

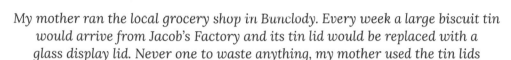

My mother ran the local grocery shop in Bunclody. Every week a large biscuit tin would arrive from Jacob's Factory and its tin lid would be replaced with a glass display lid. Never one to waste anything, my mother used the tin lids to cook the large apple tarts needed to feed our extensive family.

Serves 8-10
- 225g (8oz) plain flour
- 110g (4oz) margarine
- 150ml (¼ pint) cold water
- 5 large cooking apples, peeled, cored and sliced
- 2–3 tablespoons sugar
- 1–2 teaspoons whole cloves (optional)
- 1–2 tablespoons caster sugar

to serve
- ice-cream or cream

You will need
- large ovenproof plate

1. Preheat oven to 200°C/400°F/Gas 6.

2. Sieve flour into a bowl and rub in margarine with lightly floured hands until it resembles breadcrumbs. Add sufficient water to mix to a soft dough with a knife.

3. Turn onto a lightly floured surface and knead lightly. Roll out half the pastry to the size of an ovenproof plate and lift onto plate. Arrange apple slices on the pastry and sprinkle with sugar and cloves, if using.

4. Roll remaining pastry wide enough to cover the apples. Dampen edge of base pastry with cold water to seal, transfer the pastry onto apples and press to cover. Seal the edges with the back of a knife to form a crust, and crimp or cut at 3cm (1in) intervals to form a scalloped edge.

5. Cut a cross in the top of the pastry to allow steam to escape and bake in preheated oven for about 35 minutes or until golden. Sprinkle with caster sugar and serve hot or cold with cream or ice-cream.

Black Forest Gateau

CLAIRE ANN MCDONNELL, WICKLOW: LOVES GARDENING AND THE COUNTRY AIR

This easy cake is a favourite with all the family and makes a delicious treat for parties and gatherings, especially if you go the full mile and decorate with chocolate and crushed biscuits. We love to use Polo biscuits but you could use your personal favourites.

Serves 8–12
- 4 eggs, separated
- 110g (4oz) caster sugar
- 110g (4oz) self-raising flour
- 50g (2oz) chocolate powder
- 225g (8oz) tinned black cherries, drained, halved and stones removed
- 570ml (1 pint) cream, whipped

to finish (optional)
- grated milk chocolate
- crushed chocolate biscuits

You will need
- 2 x 20cm (8in) round sandwich tins

1. Preheat oven to 190°C/375°F/Gas 5. Line sandwich tins with baking parchment.

2. In a large mixing bowl, whisk egg whites until stiff. Sieve in the caster sugar and mix well. Add the egg yolks and mix until the mixture changes colour. Sieve in the flour and chocolate powder and gently fold in to incorporate fully.

3. Divide cake mixture between the two tins and bake in preheated oven for 12–15 minutes or until an inserted skewer comes out clean. Allow to cool in the tins for five minutes. Remove from the tins and transfer to a wire rack to cool completely.

4. Place one sponge on a serving plate and cover with a third of the cream and two thirds of the cherries. Top with the second sponge and cover the top and sides with cream.

5. Spoon the remaining cream into a piping bag. Pipe 10–12 swirls around the top and again at the base of the cake, and place a cherry on each swirl. If you like, you can finish by pressing grated chocolate or crushed chocolate biscuits to the sides of the cake with a palette knife.

6. Chill in the fridge for at least an hour before serving.

Pear & Roasted Hazelnut Tart

AN GRIANÁN, LOUTH: ICA ADULT EDUCATION CENTRE

A cross between a crumble and a cake, this delicious tart can either be served warm as a dessert or cold as a cake. It works well with many other fruits such as peaches or apricots, and you could serve with custard for some extra indulgence.

Serves 6–8
- 150g (6oz) self-raising flour
- 100g (4oz) caster sugar
- ½ teaspoon baking powder
- 100g (4oz) softened butter or margarine
- 3 eggs, lightly beaten
- 1 tablespoon crème fraîche or natural yoghurt
- 2 large ripe pears

for the topping
- 25g (1oz) softened butter
- 25g (1oz) plain flour
- 25g (1oz) brown sugar
- 1 tablespoon toasted hazelnuts

to serve
- crème fraîche or natural yoghurt

You will need
- 23cm (9in) cake tin

1. Preheat oven to 190°C/375°F/Gas 5. Grease and base-line cake tin (placing a single piece of parchment on the base only).

2. To make the topping, rub the butter into the flour until it resembles fine breadcrumbs. Mix in the sugar and hazelnuts and set aside.

3. In a large mixing bowl or food processor, combine the flour, sugar, baking powder, butter, eggs and crème fraîche and beat lightly for one minute until smooth. Pour into prepped tin.

4. Core and slice the pears and arrange on top of the cake mix. Sprinkle the hazelnut mixture over the top. Bake in a preheated oven for 35–40 minutes or until an inserted skewer comes out clean.

5. Serve hot or cold with extra crème fraîche or natural yoghurt.

ICA Tip
This is a basic all-in-one cake mix, making it a cinch to whip up in a food processor.

Almond Slices

PAULINE O'CALLAGHAN, CORK: GOLF-MAD GRANDMOTHER OF 12

My mother's maiden aunt baked excellent cakes and loved to take over the kitchen at Christmas. We used to store eggs in a horrible white solution to save them for the Christmas baking. Mammy thought she had the excuse for Auntie Maisie: "There are no eggs for baking." But the quick reply came back: "Almond slices only take one egg."

Makes 20 slices
- 175g (6oz) self-raising flour
- 110g (4oz) caster sugar
- 1 teaspoon baking powder
- 3oz margarine
- 1 egg, separated
- 3–4 tablespoons milk
- 4–5 tablespoons apricot jam
- 85g (3oz) whole almonds (or almond flakes)

You will need
- Swiss roll tray

1. Preheat oven to 140°C/275°F/Gas 1. Grease the Swiss roll tray.

2. If you're stuck for time you could use almond flakes but chopping them yourself gets the best result. If you are using whole almonds, immerse in boiling water to blanch, remove skins and chop lengthways. Set aside.

3. Combine flour, baking powder and half the sugar. Rub in margarine until it resembles breadcrumbs. Make a well in the dry ingredients, beat the egg yolk with a little milk and mix in to bind the dry ingredients.

4. Roll out the dough to about half the size of the tray, transfer and press out with finger tips to cover all of tray. Spread jam over the dough base. Beat the egg white until stiff and fold in the remaining sugar. Spread over jam and sprinkle with the chopped almonds.

5. Bake in preheated oven for 20–25 minutes or until the meringue is stiff and light brown. Allow to cool in tray and cut into 20 slices.

Fraughan Buns

CONNIE MCEVOY, LOUTH: RETIRED FARMER AND CRAFT EXPERT

At the end of a day helping our father dig for potatoes we'd pick fraughans, putting them in my father's cap and bringing them home to my mother. Today we still gather wild blueberries for these special buns from the acidic soil at the foothills of Mount Leinster.

Makes 12
- 110g (4oz) butter or margarine
- 110g (4oz) sugar
- 175g (6oz) flour
- 1 teaspoon baking powder
- pinch of salt
- 2 eggs
- 1 tablespoon milk
- 1 tablespoon sherry or cider
- 175g (6oz) fraughans (wild blueberries)

You will need
- 12-cup patty tin
- 12 baking cases

1. Preheat oven to 180°C/350°F/Gas 4.

2. Cream butter and sugar in a medium-sized bowl. In a separate bowl, sieve the flour, baking powder and salt together. Add about two tablespoons of this flour mix to the creamed butter and sugar and stir in lightly with a wooden spoon.

3. In a third bowl, beat eggs, milk and sherry together. Stir this liquid into the main mixing bowl before adding the remaining flour. The final mixture should be soft enough to drop from a spoon.

4. Wash the fraughans and dry on kitchen paper before carefully stirring through the bun mixture.

5. Line 12 patty tins with baking cases and drop a heaped teaspoon of the mixture into each one. Bake in preheated oven for about 20–25 minutes and transfer to a wire tray to cool.

Parsnip Cake with Walnuts & Raisins

ANNE GABBETT, LIMERICK: DAIRY FARMER'S WIFE AND HOME ECONOMICS TEACHER

This cake came about from a seasonal surplus of parsnips from the garden. I decided to try baking them into a cake much along the lines of a carrot cake. It turned out delicious and is now a family favourite.

Makes 2 x 900g (2lb) loaves

- 300g (10½oz) parsnips, peeled
- 250g (9oz) soft butter or margarine
- 125g (4½oz) soft brown sugar
- 125g (4½oz) caster sugar
- 3–4 drops vanilla extract
- 350g plain flour
- 2 teaspoons baking powder
- 2 teaspoons ground cinnamon
- pinch of salt
- 4 eggs, beaten
- 200g golden sultanas
- 125g walnuts, chopped
- ½ teaspoon freshly grated nutmeg

for the topping (optional)

- 125g (4½oz) cream cheese
- 50g (2oz) butter
- 250g (9oz) icing sugar, sieved
- 125g (4½oz) walnuts, chopped
- 2 tablespoons apricot jam
- ½ teaspoon ground cinnamon

You will need

- 2 x 900g (2lb) cake tins

1. Preheat oven to 180°C/350°F/Gas 4. Grease two loaf tins or line with baking parchment.

2. Finely grate the parsnips and set aside. Cream butter or margarine with both sugars and vanilla extract until light and fluffy. In a separate bowl, sieve together the flour, baking powder, cinnamon and salt.

3. Mix about a quarter of the beaten eggs to the creamed butter and sugar, and then fold in some of the flour mix. Continue, alternating egg and flour mix, until all combined. Fold in grated parsnips, sultanas, walnuts and nutmeg, mix well and pour into prepped loaf tins.

4. Place in centre of preheated oven and bake for 35–40 minutes, until the centre springs back when touched or an inserted skewer comes out clean. Allow to rest in tins for 10 minutes before transferring to a wire tray to cool.

5. To make the topping, beat cream cheese, butter and sieved icing sugar until light and spreadable. Mix in chopped walnuts. Once the cakes have cooled completely, spread with apricot jam and then with cream cheese mixture. Finish with a sprinkling of ground cinnamon.

ICA Tip
This mix also makes delicious muffins, which will bake in about 20 minutes.

Cake in a Mug

MURIEL KERR, LEITRIM: FUN-LOVING GRANNY

This quick-fix treat is a big hit with children, allowing you to whip up an individual chocolate cake in three minutes. It's also a delicious dessert for somebody who lives alone and fancies a little bit of chocolate heaven. I make it in a one-pint pyrex jug but a large mug does the trick.

Serves 1
- 4 dessertspoons flour
- 4 dessertspoons sugar
- 2 dessertspoons cocoa
- 1 small egg, beaten
- 3 dessertspoons milk
- 3 dessertspoons light oil
- 2–3 drops vanilla extract
- 1 handful chocolate chips

You will need
- large mug or 480ml (1 pint) pyrex jug
- microwave

1. Combine flour, sugar and cocoa in a mug. Stir in the egg, milk and oil, then add vanilla drops and chocolate chips.

2. Cook uncovered in the microwave on high (1,000W) for three minutes.

3. Allow to cool, tip out on to a plate and tuck in.

Coffee Mud Cake

ANNE PAYNE, LAOIS: RETIRED TEACHER WHO LOVES TRYING NEW CRAFTS

I picked up this recipe in Australia where I lived for over 30 years and I still like to bake it on a regular basis. It makes a great party cake, but be warned – it's very rich so a little goes a long way.

Serves 10
- 375ml (12fl oz) milk
- 1–2 tablespoons instant coffee
- 250g (9oz) butter
- 110g (4oz) white chocolate
- 110g (4oz) milk chocolate
- 375g (13oz) sugar
- 3 eggs, lightly beaten
- 1 teaspoon vanilla extract
- 100g (4oz) self-raising flour
- 300g (10oz) plain flour

to serve
- fresh pouring cream

You will need
- 23cm (9in) round tin

1. Preheat oven to 150°C/300°F/Gas 2. Grease a 23cm (9in) round tin and line with baking paper.

2. Heat a little of the milk, add coffee granules and dissolve thoroughly. Set aside.

3. Combine butter, white and milk chocolates, sugar and the remaining milk in a saucepan and melt over low heat. Pour into a large mixing bowl, add the dissolved coffee and allow to cool slightly before and stirring in eggs, vanilla and flour.

4. Pour mixture into prepared cake tin and bake for 1½–2 hours until it has developed a thick sugary crust and an inserted skewer comes out clean. Allow to cool in tin and serve with fresh cream.

Mince Pies

MARIE MCGUIRK, LOUTH: COOKERY TUTOR AND ASPIRING GOLFER

These mince pies have been given a tropical twist with the addition of a little pineapple and a coconut topping. They can be a nice way to convince youngsters to try mince pies, but you could always fill some of the pastry cases with raspberry or apricot jam instead.

Makes about 24
- 225g (8oz) self-raising flour, plus a little extra
- 110g (4oz) cold butter, roughly chopped
- 50g (2oz) caster sugar
- 1 egg, beaten
- 450g (1lb) luxury mincemeat
- 140g (5oz) tinned pineapple, cut into small chunks

for the topping
- 110g (4oz) soft butter
- 110g (4oz) caster sugar
- 2 eggs
- 1 tablespoon plain flour
- 175g (6oz) desiccated coconut

to finish
- 4 tablespoons desiccated coconut

You will need
- 2 x 12-cup bun tins
- scone cutter

1. Preheat oven to 180°C/350°F/Gas 4. Lightly grease the bun tins.

2. Rub butter into flour until it resembles fine breadcrumbs, mix in sugar and bind with beaten egg to form a soft pastry dough.

3. Knead pastry on a lightly floured surface until smooth and divide in four. Roll out one quarter of the pastry and cut out circles with a scone cutter. Place the circles in bun tins, repeating until all the pastry is gone.

4. To make the topping, combine the soft butter, sugar, flour, eggs and coconut in a mixing bowl and beat together.

5. Fill each pastry case with a teaspoon of mincemeat, add a piece of pineapple and top with a teaspoon of the cake mix topping. Sprinkle with coconut and bake in preheated oven for 15 minutes or until nicely golden and heated through.

6. Remove from the oven and allow to cool in baking tin for five minutes before removing onto a cooling tray to cool fully.

Fruit Cake

EILEEN MCGLEW, LOUTH: GRAN WHO LOVES TRYING NEW RECIPES

I've tried many fruit cake recipes over the years. This is my favourite and always makes an appearance on my table when visitors come for tea. I even use it as Christmas cake. It is as lovely with a glass of cold milk as with a cup of hot tea.

Serves 8–10
- 225g (8oz) sultanas
- 225g (8oz) raisins
- 100g (4oz) mixed peel
- 100g (4oz) light brown sugar
- 175g (6oz) butter
- 175ml (6fl oz) water
- 225g (8oz) plain flour
- 1 teaspoon bicarbonate of soda
- ½ teaspoon ground ginger
- 3 eggs, beaten
- 2 tablespoons rum

You will need
- 20cm (8in) cake tin

ICA Tip

It really is worth sourcing quality fruit for this recipe, they'll make it all the more delicious.

1. Preheat oven to 180°C/350°F/Gas 4. Lightly grease cake tin and line with baking parchment.

2. Boil fruit, sugar and butter with water for five minutes, stirring frequently. Remove from heat and set aside to cool.

3. Sieve flour, soda and ground ginger into a large mixing bowl. Pour in the boiled fruit mixture and mix well. Add the eggs and rum and beat well.

4. Transfer the mixture to prepped cake tin and bake in preheated oven for 90 minutes or until an inserted skewer comes out clean. Allow to cool in the tin. Once fully cooled, wrap in greaseproof paper and store in airtight container where it will keep well.

Carrot & Pineapple Squares

AN GRIANÁN, LOUTH: ICA ADULT EDUCATION CENTRE

This is a nice twist on a basic carrot cake recipe, with the pineapple adding an extra sweetness. A perfect afternoon pick-me-up with a pot of tea.

Makes 12
- 275g (10oz) soft brown sugar
- 225ml (8fl oz) vegetable oil
- 4 eggs, beaten
- 150g (5oz) plain flour
- 150g (5oz) wholemeal flour
- 2 teaspoons bicarbonate of soda
- 2 teaspoons ground cinnamon
- 225g (8oz) carrots, peeled and coarsely grated
- 400g (14oz) tinned unsweetened crushed pineapple, drained
- 75g (3oz) chopped walnuts

for the glaze
- 175g (6oz) icing sugar, sieved
- 1–2 tablespoons lemon juice, to taste

You will need
- 23cm x 32.5cm (9in x 13in) shallow tin

1. Preheat oven to 180°C/350°F/Gas 4. Grease shallow tin.

2. Combine brown sugar, oil and eggs into a large mixing bowl and blend well. Sieve in the flours, soda and cinnamon, and then fold in any bran remaining in the sieve. Stir with a wooden spoon to blend and beat to a smooth batter.

3. Fold in the carrot, pineapple and walnuts and mix well. Pour mixture into the prepped tin and spread level. Bake in preheated oven for 45–60 minutes or until an inserted skewer comes out clean.

4. Meanwhile to make the glaze, combine the sieved icing sugar with sufficient lemon juice to make a smooth icing.

5. Once the cake is cooked, allow to cool completely in baking tin. Spoon the lemon glaze over the surface with a wet knife and allow to set. When set, cut the cake into squares and lift from the tin as required.

Strawberry Sablé

AN GRIANÁN, LOUTH: ICA ADULT EDUCATION CENTRE

Susie McCulloch, our pastry cook in An Grianán, has made this her signature dish and it is a favourite with all the guests. Sablé are fairly straightforward to make and are perfect for a summer party. You can get creative with how you serve them, opting for a second layer in the classic style or even serving as an open strawberry sandwich.

Makes about 8–10
- 175g (6oz) butter
- 125g (4½oz) sugar
- 3 egg yolks
- 250g (9oz) plain flour
- 50g (2oz) ground almonds

for the filling
- 625ml (1¼ pints) cream
- 30g (1oz) icing sugar
- 1 punnet strawberries, husked

You will need
- baking sheet or tray
- 6cm (2½in) diameter cookie cutter

1. Preheat oven to 180°C/350°F/Gas 4. Line baking sheet or tray with baking parchment.

2. In a food processor cream sugar and butter together until light and fluffy. Add egg yolks and mix well to combine before sieving in flour and ground almonds. Mix gently until it binds together to form a pastry dough.

3. Turn pastry onto a lightly floured surface, roll out and cut into circles with cookie cutter. Transfer to parchment-lined baking tray and prick the centre of each biscuit with a skewer so they don't rise. Bake in preheated oven for 10 minutes, or until light golden in colour. Remove and allow to cool fully on the parchment.

4. Meanwhile, whisk the cream and icing sugar for the filling, and slice the strawberries thinly. When the biscuits have cooled, spread half with cream, layer with strawberry slices and top with a second biscuit. Dust with icing sugar.

Anzac Biscuits

ANNE PAYNE, LAOIS: RETIRED TEACHER WHO LOVES TRYING NEW CRAFTS

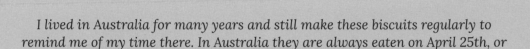

I lived in Australia for many years and still make these biscuits regularly to remind me of my time there. In Australia they are always eaten on April 25th, or Anzac Day, to remember Australian Troops who served in World War I.

Makes about 40 biscuits
- 225g (8oz) sugar
- 175g (6oz) rolled oats
- 200g (7oz) plain flour
- 250g (9oz) butter
- 2 tablespoons golden syrup
- 1 teaspoon bicarbonate of soda

You will need
- baking sheet or tray

1. Preheat oven to 150°C/300°F/Gas 2. Grease a baking sheet or tray.

2. Combine sugar, rolled oats and flour in a mixing bowl. In a small bowl, melt syrup in a little hot water, add butter and when melted stir in the soda. Add to the dry ingredients and mix well to form a stickie cookie dough.

3. Lightly flour your hands and roll about a teaspoon each of dough into round balls. Place these on a greased baking tray – they should be well-spaced as they will flatten out as they cook.

4. Bake in preheated oven for 15–20 minutes or until golden brown. Allow to cool fully on the baking tray.

Dried Fruit Salad

AUDREY STARRETT, DONEGAL: JACK OF ALL TRADES

Simple, healthy and very very tasty, this salad uses dried fruit from your storecupboard and transforms them into a versatile dish that is as good to start a day with as it is to finish a meal with.

Serves 10–12
- 110g (4oz) prunes, de-stoned and chopped
- 110g (4oz) dried apricots, chopped
- 110g (4oz) dried figs, hard stalks removed and chopped
- 110g (4oz) large raisins
- 550ml (1 pint) cold water
- 1 orange, zest and juice
- 50g (2oz) hazelnuts
- 150ml (5fl oz) cream
- 150ml (5fl oz) natural yoghurt

ICA Tip
This will keep well in the fridge and can be made a day or two in advance to allow the flavours develop.

1. Soak the fruit overnight in cold water.

2. The next day simmer for about 10 minutes or until tender. Stir in the orange juice and zest. Tip into a glass bowl and leave to cool before covering with clingfilm and chilling for at least an hour.

3. Meanwhile, roast the hazelnuts in a dry frying pan on the stovetop, under a hot grill or in a hot oven. Either way, watch them closely to catch them when browned and aromatic but before they burn. Chop roughly.

4. Just before serving, whip the cream and fold in the yoghurt. Pour over the fruit and serve sprinkled with chopped hazelnuts.

Chocolate Coffee Mousse Cups

AN GRIANÁN, LOUTH: ICA ADULT EDUCATION CENTRE

This luscious dessert is very rich, so a little goes a long way. Served in small dishes it is a delicious way to finish a fine meal.

Serves 6
- 110g (4oz) good quality chocolate ,
- 140g (5oz) mascarpone cheese
- 2 tablespoons icing sugar
- 2 tablespoons strong coffee
- 2 tablespoons Bailey's Irish Cream
- 150ml (¼ pint) cream
- 1 teaspoon chocolate powder

to serve
- amaretti biscuits

You will need
- 6 coffee cups or ramekins

1. Place a large heatproof bowl over a pot of boiling water and gently melt the chocolate. Set aside to cool a little but do not allow to reset.

2. Beat the mascarpone and icing sugar together and stir in the coffee and Bailey's. Fold this mixture into the cooled chocolate. Whip the cream until thick and gently fold into the chocolate mixture.

3. Pour into coffee cups or ramekin dishes. Sprinkle with chocolate powder and chill for an hour or two or overnight.

4. Serve each mousse cup with an amaretti biscuit on the side for dipping.

Pavlova

MELLA WINTERS, WEXFORD: LOVES THE CRAIC AND COUNTRY WALKS

This is such a simple recipe to make but nonetheless delicious. I make it some weekends and for special occasions and family get-togethers.

Serves 6–8
- 4 egg whites
- 225g (8oz) caster sugar
- 1 tablespoon cornflour
- 2 tablespoons white wine vinegar
- ¼ teaspoon vanilla extract
- 300ml (10fl oz) double cream
- 300g (10oz) strawberries
- 1 small fresh pineapple, peeled and cut in cubes

You will need
- baking sheet

1. Preheat oven to 150°C/300°F/Gas 2. Line a baking sheet with baking parchment.

2. Whisk the egg whites until stiff. Add the sugar one tablespoon at a time, whisking until the meringue is very stiff. Whisk in the cornflour, white wine vinegar and vanilla extract.

3. Pile the meringue onto lined baking sheet and spread into a 23cm (9in) circle. Hollow out the centre slightly and bake in preheated oven for 90 minutes.

4. Allow to cool, remove the paper and transfer to a serving dish. Whip the cream until stiff. Fold in some of the fresh fruit and pile onto the meringue. Decorate with the remaining fruit.

Easy Strawberry Cheesecake

CLAIRE ANN MCDONNELL, WICKLOW: LOVES GARDENING AND THE COUNTRY AIR

This is a favourite recipe of mine and really very easy to make. It was given to me by a friend but I like to make the addition of puréed strawberries dotted throughout the cheesecake mixture. It was a winner in the Wicklow Federation Competition in 2011.

Serves 8
- 300g digestive biscuits
- 50g (2oz) butter, melted
- 135g (5oz) packet of strawberry jelly
- 125g (4½oz) strawberry yoghurt
- 275ml (½ pint) boiling water
- 275ml (½ pint) cream, whipped
- 225g (8oz) cream cheese
- 1 small punnet strawberries, husked
- 1 small handful picked mint leaves (optional)

You will need
- 25cm (10in) springform tin

1. Crush the biscuits and mix well with melted butter. Press into the base of tin and refrigerate until ready to use.

2. Dilute the jelly in boiling water and set aside to cool a little. Combine the cheese and yoghurt and mix into a paste. Add the cream and gently whisk in the diluted jelly, mixing well. Remove the base from the fridge and pour the cheese mixture over it.

3. Mash some of the strawberries in a small bowl and dot them here and there through the mixture. Return the cheesecake to the fridge to set, about an hour.

4. To finish, slice the remaining strawberries to decorate the top and sides of the cheesecake and garnish with mint leaves.

Blackberry & Apple Crumble

MARGARET O'REILLY, CORK: PRIZE-WINNING MAKER OF CARRICKMACROSS LACE

This is based on a recipe for apple tartlet with walnuts which I played around with. The result is a very enjoyable way to finish a dinner party. I have been cooking this for years and still love its combination of flavours.

Serves 6–8
- 65g (2½oz) butter
- 175g (6oz) fresh white breadcrumbs
- 50g (2oz) soft brown sugar
- 60ml (2fl oz) golden syrup
- 2 lemons, finely grated zest and juice
- 50g (2oz) ground almonds
- 50g (2oz) chopped almonds
- 450g (1lb) blackberries
- 450g (1lb) cooking apples, peeled, cored and finely sliced

for the custard
- 2 tablespoons custard powder
- 1–2 tablespoons sugar
- 575ml (1 pint) milk

You will need
- 450ml (¾ pint) ovenproof dish

1. Preheat oven to 180°C/350°F/Gas 4. Grease ovenproof dish with a knob of butter.

2. Melt the remaining butter in a frying pan and sauté the breadcrumbs for about five minutes or until crisp and golden. Set aside to cool.

3. Combine the sugar, syrup, lemon zest and juice in a small saucepan and gently warm through. Add the breadcrumbs together with the ground and chopped almonds and mix well.

4. Arrange a thin layer of blackberries in the base of the dish, top with a thin layer of crumb mixture, another of apples and another layer of crumbs. Repeat the process, alternating apples and berries until all used up and finishing with a layer of crumbs. The mixture should be piled well above the top of the dish as it will shrink during cooking. Bake in preheated oven for 30 minutes until the crumbs are golden and fruit is soft.

5. Meanwhile in a large mixing bowl, combine the custard powder and sugar and mix to a smooth paste with a couple of tablespoons of milk. Heat the remaining milk to almost boiling and pour over the custard mix, stirring well. Return to the saucepan over a gentle heat and bring back to almost boiling, stirring continuously.

6. Serve the crumble warm accompanied by a jug of hot custard.

Australian Paradise Meringues

ADA VANCE, CAVAN: HILL-WALKING GRANNY AND EXPERT PATCHWORKER

I visited Australia a while back and a friend gave me this recipe which I since tweaked to make my own. It won second prize in the ICA Gempack Competition 2011 and is always a popular treat in my house.

Makes 8
- 3 large egg whites
- 110g (4oz) soft dark brown sugar
- 25g (1oz) caster sugar
- 25g (1oz) icing sugar
- 1 dessertspoon cornflour
- 1 dessertspoon malt vinegar

for the filling
- 50g (2oz) dark chocolate
- 85g (3oz) crème fraîche

to serve
- 100g (3½oz) flaked almonds (optional)
- 1 tablespoon cocoa powder

You will need
- baking tray

ICA Tip
A bain marie can be used to melt chocolate over an indirect heat. Simply place a heatproof bowl over a pot of simmering water.

1. Preheat oven to 130°C/250°F/Gas ½. Line baking tray with parchment paper.

2. In a large mixing bowl, whisk egg whites until they form stiff peaks. Gradually add brown sugar, whisking all the time. Fold in the caster sugar. Sieve over the icing sugar and cornflour and fold this in.

3. Quickly mix in the vinegar and pile 16 spoonfuls onto lined baking tray (or pipe with large nozzle). Bake for two hours in the low oven, by which stage they should lift off easily and not feel sticky. Allow to cool on a wire rack.

4. Meanwhile, toast the almond flakes in a dry frying pan, in the oven or under the grill, taking care to catch them before they burn. Melt chocolate over gentle heat (see Tip) or in microwave. Cool a little before beating in the crème fraîche.

5. Sandwich pairs of cooled meringue with the chocolate crème fraîche, sprinkle with toasted almonds and serve with a light dusting of cocoa powder.

Tropical Baked Rice Queen of Puddings

BREDA MCDONALD, KILKENNY: PASSIONATE BELIEVER IN LOCAL COMMUNITY

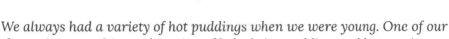

We always had a variety of hot puddings when we were young. One of our favourites was this combination of baked rice pudding and hot meringue flavoured with home-made raspberry jam. I've added coconut to give the meringue a nice crispness.

Serves 6
- 100g (4oz) pudding rice (pearl rice)
- 50g (2oz) caster sugar
- 900ml (1½ pint) milk
- 75ml (3fl oz) cream

for the topping
- 3 egg whites
- 175g (6oz) caster sugar
- 4 tablespoons raspberry jam
- 1 dessertspoon Demerara sugar
- 1 dessertspoon desiccated coconut

to serve
- freshly whipped cream

You will need
- large casserole dish

1. Preheat oven to 180°C/350°F/Gas 4.

2. To make the rice pudding, combine the rice, sugar and milk in a medium-sized saucepan and slowly bring to the boil over a gentle heat, stirring regularly to stop the rice from sticking. Reduce the heat, add the cream and allow to simmer for 15 minutes on a very low heat.

3. Pour the mixture into a large casserole dish and bake in preheated oven for 15 minutes or until a skin forms on the top of the pudding.

4. Meanwhile rapidly whisk the egg whites in a clean mixing bowl until stiffly beaten. Gradually add the caster sugar and whisk until the mixture is glossy and has formed stiff peaks. If turned upside down the mixture should remain in the bowl.

5. Remove the pudding from the oven and spread with raspberry jam. Spoon over the meringue topping and spread roughly around the top of the pudding. Sprinkle with the brown sugar and coconut and return to the oven for 10–15 minutes until golden and crispy. Serve immediately with lots of freshly whipped cream.

Blueberry Bread Pudding

AN GRIANÁN, LOUTH: ICA ADULT EDUCATION CENTRE

A very traditional pudding given a modern twist, this is a hot favourite at An Grianán and is delicious served warm with vanilla ice-cream. You could play around with whatever fruit is in season: raspberries in summer or blackberries in autumn, maybe with some chopped apple.

Serves 4–6

- 6 mini pain au lait (or 4 thick slices sweet bread or barn brack)
- 3 eggs
- 3 tablespoons caster sugar
- 1 teaspoon vanilla extract
- 425ml (¾ pint) milk
- 250g (9oz) blueberries
- 25g (1oz) flaked almonds

to serve

- vanilla ice-cream, Greek-style yoghurt or fresh cream

You will need

- baking sheet
- shallow ovenproof dish

1. Preheat oven to 190°C/375°F/Gas 5. Place a baking sheet in oven to heat. Grease a shallow ovenproof dish.

2. Cut bread into chunks, place on preheated baking sheet and bake in preheated oven for about 10 minutes until lightly browned. Set aside to cool.

3. Beat together the eggs, sugar, vanilla and milk. Combine bread and berries in a buttered ovenproof dish and pour over the egg mixture. Sprinkle with flaked almonds and set aside for 30 minutes before baking.

4. Bake in preheated for about 30 minutes or until golden brown and lightly set. Serve hot with vanilla ice-cream, Greek-style yoghurt or fresh cream.

Sticky Date Pudding with Pecan Toffee Sauce

AN GRIANÁN, LOUTH: ICA ADULT EDUCATION CENTRE

This is a speciality of Peter Lawlor, our head chef in An Grianán.
A rich, deep-flavoured pudding, it is comfort food at its
finest – particularly on a chilly Irish evening.

Serves 8
- 85g (3oz) butter
- 85g (3oz) caster sugar
- 2 eggs
- 175g (6oz) chopped dates
- 180ml (6fl oz) boiling water
- 1 teaspoon vanilla extract
- 2 teaspoons strong coffee
- ½ teaspoon bicarbonate of soda
- 175g (6oz) self-raising flour

for the sauce
- 175g (6oz) soft brown sugar
- 110g (4oz) butter
- 100ml (3½fl oz) double cream
- 1 small handful pecan nuts or walnuts, chopped

You will need
- baking tray

1. Preheat oven to 190°C/375°F/Gas 5. Lightly grease a baking tray.

2. In a large mixing bowl, cream butter and sugar together. Add beaten eggs a little at a time, beating to incorporate.

3. Pour boiling water over chopped dates, add vanilla, coffee and soda and mix well. Fold into creamed butter mixture, and fold in flour. Pour into baking tray and bake in preheated oven for 25 minutes. Allow to cool for five minutes before turning out.

4. To make the sauce, combine sugar, butter, cream and nuts in a pan over a low heat. Bring to boiling point very slowly and serve with the warm date pudding.

White Chocolate Bread & Butter Pudding

EDWARD HAYDEN, KILKENNY: TV CHEF AND FOOD WRITER

Although enriched with chocolate and soaked sultanas, at its heart this recipe remains true to the traditional style of bread and butter pudding, which was a staple dessert beloved in Ireland for many years before deep freezers negated the need to use up stale bread.

Serves 6–8
- 1 loaf white bread, sliced (about 12–16 slices)
- 110g (4oz) butter
- 200g (7oz) caster sugar
- 75g (3oz) sultanas, rinsed in hot water
- 4 tablespoons orange juice or whiskey (optional)
- 500ml (16fl oz) milk
- 100ml (3½fl oz) cream
- 5 large eggs
- 110g (4oz) white chocolate, finely chopped (or chocolate drops)
- ¼ teaspoon ground cinnamon
- 50g (2oz) flaked almonds (optional)

for the butterscotch sauce
- 50g (2oz) butter
- 50g (2oz) dark brown sugar
- 200ml (7fl oz) cream

to serve
- fresh cream

You will need
- 25cm (10in) ovenproof dish

1. Preheat oven to 180°C/350°F/Gas 4. Lightly grease ovenproof dish.

2. Butter the bread and cut off the crusts, and set aside about a quarter of the sugar for layering through the bread. Soak the rinsed sultanas in orange juice or whiskey for 30 minutes, if using, and drain well.

3. In a large saucepan, gently heat the milk and cream bringing them almost to the boil.

4. Layer the bread into greased dish, scattering a layer of sultanas and a little sugar between each layer of bread. Finish with a top layer of bread.

5. Beat the eggs in a large mixing bowl with the remaining sugar until combined. Add the white chocolate and cinnamon.

6. Pour the boiled milk and cream over the egg and chocolate mixture and whisk well until combined. Slowly pour all of this mixture over the buttered bread and set aside for about 10 minutes to soak. Scatter the flaked almonds on top and bake in preheated oven for 40 minutes, until the pudding is well risen and almost set to the touch.

7. To make the butterscotch sauce, melt the butter and brown sugar in a small saucepan until bubbling point. Whisk in the pouring cream and simmer for five minutes. Serve the pudding hot with butterscotch sauce and cream.

ICA Tip
You can have the pudding assembled and soaked in advance and leave it in the fridge until you are ready to cook it.

Cranberry & Chocolate Roulade

BRID MALONE, LAOIS: MOTHER OF FIVE, WALKER AND SWIMMER

The tart cranberries give this chocolate roulade a refreshing edge after a rich meal. I like to serve it after my Christmas dinner of roast goose with damson sauce (see p62) but really it is delicious any time of year. This recipe won me first prize in the 1998 ICA All-Ireland Christmas Recipe Competition.

Serves 8–10
- 4 eggs, separated
- 140g (5oz) sugar
- 40g (1½oz) cocoa powder

for the filling
- 225g (8oz) fresh cranberries (or frozen, defrosted fully)
- 3 tablespoons orange juice
- 85g (3oz) caster sugar
- 275ml (½ pint) cream, whipped stiffly
- 2 tablespoons Grand Marnier

to garnish
- icing sugar
- sprig of holly
- mixed frozen berries defrosted (optional)

You will need
- 20cm x 30cm (8in x 12in) Swiss roll tin

1. Preheat oven to 180°C/350°F/Gas 4. Grease Swiss roll tin and line with baking parchment.

2. In a large bowl, whisk egg yolks with sugar until pale in colour and very thick and light in texture. Sieve over the cocoa and gently fold in using a metal spoon.

3. Whisk the egg whites until just stiff but not dry. Fold a third of this into the roulade mix. Repeat with the second third, and finally fold in the remaining egg white. Pour into prepared tin and bake in preheated oven for 18–20 minutes or until well risen and springy to touch. Cover with a damp tea towel and leave to cool in tin.

4. To make the filling, gently simmer the cranberries, orange juice and sugar in a saucepan for about 10 minutes or until tender. Remove from the heat and allow to cool before folding into the whipped cream together with the Grand Marnier.

5. Turn the cooled roulade onto a sheet of baking parchment dusted with icing sugar. Trim the edges and spread the cream mixture over the roulade. Roll up gently but don't worry if it cracks slightly.

6. Chill for at least two hours before serving. Dust with more icing sugar and decorate with defrosted berries and a sprig of holly.

Egg-Free Christmas Pudding

MARY FITZGERALD, WEXFORD: GARDENER AND INTERNET ENTHUSIAST

I make my Christmas puddings in the autumn mid-term break every year. If you want to make this recipe gluten-free, you could use gluten-free flour, baking powder and breadcrumbs. You could substitute some of the fruit for dried dates or a tropical fruit mix.

Makes 4 medium-sized puddings
- 340g (12oz) breadcrumbs
- 340g (12oz) brown sugar
- 340g (12oz) raisins
- 340g (12oz) sultanas
- 340g (12oz) currants
- 110g (4oz) candied peel
- 2 cooking apples, peeled, cored and grated
- 1 large carrot, peeled and grated
- 1 lemon, finely grated rind
- 1 orange, finely grated rind
- 1 teaspoon ground cloves
- 1 teaspoon mixed spice
- 170g (6oz) butter, melted
- 500ml (17fl oz) stout
- 3 teaspoons baking powder

to finish
- 2 tablespoons rum or brandy per pudding

to serve
- brandy butter, cream, custard or ice-cream

You will need
- 4 medium-sized pudding bowls, or one large and two smaller
- cotton twine

1. Mix together all dry ingredients except baking powder, add the melted butter and enough of the stout to moisten well and bring to a thick porridge-like consistency, reserving the remaining stout. Stir very well and leave overnight to soak.

2. The next day, add baking powder and mix well. Check the consistency, which should be fairly stiff but loose enough to drop off a spoon, and adjust by add more stout if too dry or more breadcrumbs if too moist.

3. Lightly grease several pudding bowls and fill each up to about 3cm (1in) from the top. Cover with a double circle of greaseproof paper and then with a lid of double kitchen foil tightened with cotton twine under the rim.

4. Place each pudding into a saucepan of simmering water, cover and steam for eight hours. The water should come half way up the bowl, and will need to be topped up periodically.

5. Once cooked, remove puddings from water, remove paper and foil covers, and pour two tablespoons of rum or brandy over each of the hot puddings. Allow to cool overnight and then recover with fresh greaseproof paper and foil, and store in a cool place until needed.

6. When serving, either tip the pudding onto a serving plate and flame with brandy or simply slice from the bowl. Serve hot or cold with brandy butter, cream, custard or ice-cream.

ICA Tip

These steamed puddings will keep indefinitely. They are traditionally made in October or early November so that the flavour is well-developed by Christmas.

Bailey's Cheesecake

AN GRIANÁN, LOUTH: ICA ADULT EDUCATION CENTRE

Our head chef, Peter Lawlor, likes to add a splash of Irish whiskey to intensify the flavour. You can tone down the booziness to make it more family-friendly if you prefer.

Serves 8
- 300g digestive biscuits
- 3–4 ginger nut biscuits (optional)
- 85g (3oz) butter, melted
- 450g (1lb) cream cheese
- 225g (8oz) caster sugar
- 5 gelatine leaves
- 275ml (½ pint) milk
- 85ml (3fl oz) Bailey's Irish Cream
- 30ml (1fl oz) Irish whiskey (optional)
- 2 tablespoons strong coffee (optional)
- 275ml (½ pint) cream, whipped

to finish
- whipped cream
- grated chocolate

You will need
- 21cm (9in) round tin

ICA *Tip*
Baking the base of the cheesecake for a few minutes helps to make it firmer and less likely to crumble when serving.

1. Preheat oven to 170°C/325°F/Gas 3. Allow the cream cheese to come to room temperature.

2. Crush the biscuits roughly and mix well with melted butter. Press into tin with potato masher and bake for five minutes in preheated oven. Remove and allow to cool.

3. Cream together the cheese and sugar. Soften the gelatine leaves in a little water for about five minutes.

4. Heat the milk in a small saucepan and add the softened gelatine, stirring to dissolve. Allow to cool fully before stirring in the cream cheese, Bailey's, whiskey and coffee, if using. Gently fold in whipped cream.

5. Fold onto prepared base and refrigerate to set for at least two hours. Decorate with swirls of cream and grated chocolate.

Appendices

Useful Equipment & Glossary
Recipe Contributors
Historic Members of the ICA
Acknowledgements
List of Photographs

Useful Equipment
& Glossary

A FEW WORDS ABOUT TEMPERATURES AND MEASUREMENTS

Note that temperatures given throughout this book are for conventional ovens.
If you have a fan oven, reduce the suggested temperature by about 20°C (eg from 200°C to 180°C).
Note that all teaspoon measurements are for a level teaspoon, unless otherwise specified. All
tablespoon measurements are for tablespoon, not dessertspoon unless otherwise specified.
Both metric and imperial measurements have been provided. It is best to follow one or the other, as in
some cases they have been rounded up or down (1oz = 28g, not 25g) for practicality of use.

Useful Equipment

Baking parchment: also known as silicone paper, baking paper or greaseproof paper, this is essential for many baking recipes in order to line the tins.

Baking sheet: a flat baking sheet (as opposed to shallow baking tray) is very useful for baking certain breads and cakes, and can be preheated for optimum results.

Blender: a stand-alone electrical appliance used for chopping, mixing or liquidising foods.

Bun tin: also known as a patty tin, this is a baking tray with six, nine or 12 cup depressions for making buns and mini pies.

Cake tin: cake tins come in various sizes and shapes. If using a square tin rather than a round one, reduce the dimensions by 2.5cm (1in).

Casserole: a large ovenproof lidded dish for cooking large stews in the oven or on the stovetop.

Chopping board: it is good practice to allocate one chopping board to dealing with raw meats and fish, another for vegetables including pungent onions and garlic, and another for fruits and bread. Always wash in hot soapy water after dealing with raw meat and fish.

Flan tin: also known as a quiche tin or tart tin, these will often have a removable base.

Food processor: a multi-functional appliance that has a container and a number of different removable revolving blades, which allows food to be cut, sliced, shredded, blended, beaten or liquidised.

Frying pan: whether you have a modern non-stick frying pan or an old-fashioned cast iron style, the weight of the pan is important; a heavy-based pan will distribute heat more evenly and be less likely to burn food.

Grater: a good grater is a real friend in the kitchen; look for one with several grades of fineness or invest in a selection of quality graters.

Hand-blender: also known as a billy, a hand-held electrical appliance useful for liquidising, blending or puréeing foods such as soups without transferring from the cooking vessel.

Loaf tin: tins for breadmaking are usually defined by the volume they hold rather than their shape (eg 900g / 2lb loaf tin).

Measuring jug: a plastic, pyrex or glass jug for measuring liquids; it is worth having both metric and imperial measurements as well as American cups.

Measuring spoons: stainless-steel collection of spoons, including teaspoons and tablespoons; useful to have for baking as many households no longer have a full-sized tablespoon in their cutlery set.

Melon baller: useful for balling melon or potatoes and for coring apples and pears.

Mixer: a stand-alone electrical appliance with interchangeable blades; useful for everything from folding and whipping to beating and mixing ingredients.

Palette knife: useful for smoothing surfaces and for loosening and lifting cakes from baking tins.

Pastry brush: choose a silicone one which is easy to wash.

Peeler: life is too short to use a bad peeler; there are various versions out there so experiment and when you find one that works for you, hold on to it.

Pestle & mortar: granite, ceramic or wooden bowl (mortar) with accompanying handheld utensil for grinding or crushing ingredients.

Piping bag: handy for decorating cakes with precision.

Ramekin: individual round ceramic dishes useful for making various pies and puddings.

Roasting rack: also known as a trivet, this is a little metal stand on which you can sit ingredients into a roasting tin without touching the base of tin; useful for roasting fatty poultry such as duck or goose.

Rolling pin: a good rolling pin is essential for baking with pastry; some like to use a ceramic one to keep the pastry extra cool.

Scone cutter: also known as pastry cutter or cookie cutter, it is useful to have a variety of sizes for use in all sorts of baking.

Sieve: it is worth having a general sieve for use with dry ingredients when baking as well as a colander (for draining wet ingredients) and perhaps a fine chinoise for passing purées.

Skewers: a metal skewer is very useful in judging if food is cooked, from meats and fish to cakes and baking.

Slow cooker: also known as a crock pot, this stand-alone appliance is ideal for very slow, unsupervised cooking.

Spring-form tin: tin for baking with adjustable sides which allow the tin to be easily removed.

Thermometer: sugar or jam thermometers may be worth investing in if you plan on making a lot of jam (or see p113 for techniques on testing setting point). A meat thermometer is useful to judge the central temperature of a large joint of meat.

Weighing scales: if you like to bake, an electronic scales might be worth investing in, as they allow you measure very refined and exact weights.

Wire cooling rack: cooling rack for baking; the circulation of air is essential for forming a good crust on bread and for even cooling of cakes.

Glossary

Base-line: line a cake tin with parchment to cover the base only.

Bicarbonate of soda: also known as sodium bicarbonate, bread soda or baking soda, this differs from baking powder and requires an acid such as butter milk to activate its leavening properties.

Bind: to moisten and bring together dry ingredients with a small amount of liquid in order to form into a paste or dough.

Blanch: a technique of par-cooking vegetables; boiling briefly and then arresting the cooking in cold or iced water helps retain a firm texture and bright colour.

Blitz: to blend to a purée with a hand-blender or in a blender.

Cook's knife: a good, well-maintained knife will do much to improve your cooking; always store carefully to keep it as sharp as possible.

Crimp: a term for impressing a patterned seal on a pastry rim, this can be done with fingers, fork or knife.

Descale: to remove the scales from the skin of fish; this can be a messy business, so ask your fishmonger to do it if he hasn't already.

Dropping consistency: a baking term for a consistency loose enough to drop from a spoon.

Fillet: if buying whole fish, you can ask your fishmonger to prepare it by gutting, removing the head and removing the fish fillets from the bones.

Fold: in baking, the gentle action of folding incorporates dry ingredients such as flour or sugar into whipped ingredients such as whipped egg white or cream while retaining as much air in the whipped ingredients as possible.

Pin-boning: some fillets of fish will still have large pin-bones running down along the side of the fillet; check for these with your fingers and remove with a large flat tweezers.

Sauté: to fry vegetables such as onion very quickly in order to brown and caramelise while cooking; do not stir too often.

Sear: also known as browning, to cook meat quickly on a high heat in order to encourage caramelisation of sugars.

Sweat: to fry vegetables such as onion very slowly and gently in order to soften without browning; it helps to cover with a lid and perhaps some greaseproof paper to keep the moisture in.

Toast: nuts, seeds and spices can be toasted on a dry frying pan, under a hot grill or in a low oven in order to release aromas; watch closely to catch before they burn.

Recipe Contributors

ICA Guild Members

Ada Vance, Cavan: hill-walking granny and expert patchworker (p56 & p170)

Anna Sinnott, Wicklow: busy housewife who loves to bake (p121 & p122)

Anne Gabbett, Limerick: dairy farmer's wife and home economics teacher (p49, p89 & p151)

Anne Maria Dennison, Limerick: former ICA National President (p115 & p120)

Anne Payne, Laois: retired teacher who loves trying new crafts (p155 & p162)

Annette Dunne, Cavan: working grandmother who loves reading (p5)

Audrey Starrett, Donegal: jack of all trades (p2, p39, p94 & p163)

Breda McDonald, Kilkenny: passionate believer in local community (p22, p44, p97 & p171)

Brid Malone, Laois: mother of five, walker and swimmer (p18, p62, p88, p92, p93, p109, p110 & p176)

Caroline Power, Meath: lover of crafts and reading (p140)

Claire Ann McDonnell, Wicklow: loves gardening and the country air (p74, p90, p144 & p167)

Connie McEvoy, Louth: retired farmer and craft expert (p134 & p149)

Eileen McGlew, Louth: gran who loves trying new recipes (p157)

Gwen Carter, Westmeath: beloved mother and grandmother, RIP (p65, p96 & p111)

Joan Hatton, Wicklow: loves working with mother nature (p116)

Kathleen Gorman, Laois: baker, knitter and keen reader (p75, p114 & p131)

Kay McGuirl, Wicklow: loves to swim and walk the mini-marathon (p105)

Lily Barrett, Tipperary: loves cooking, dancing and volunteering (p79)

Liz Wall, Wicklow: busy mum and ICA National President (p6, p9, p51 & p143)

Mairead O'Carroll, Cork: mother of six who loves entertaining (p25)

Margaret O'Reilly, Cork: prize-winning maker of Carrickmacross Lace (p10, p24 & p168)

Margaret Sides, Longford: likes reading, cooking and walking (p86)

Marie O'Toole, Dublin: passionate gardener and aspiring writer (p17)

Mary Fitzgerald, Wexford: gardener and internet enthusiast (p32 & p178)

Mary Harrahill, Meath: enjoys a good céilí (p72 & p83)

Mary O'Neill, Wicklow: retired teacher with a grá for travel (p106)

Maureen Butler, Meath: bridge-playing mother of four (p55)

Maureen Quigley, Wicklow: loves to read and bake (p117 & p118)

Mella Winters, Wexford: loves the craic and country walks (p166)

Muriel Kerr, Leitrim: fun-loving granny (p152)

Norah McDermott, Kildare: fan of savoury foods (p38 & p40)

Nuala Costello, Laois: mother of four who loves to cook and bake (p8)

Patricia Acheson, Cavan: farmer and community worker (p141)

Pauline O'Callaghan, Cork: golf-mad grandmother of 12 (p148)

Rita Clohessy, Cork: sea-loving grandmother and fisherwoman (p47)

Stephanie Igoe, Longford: volunteer and busy mum of three (p15, p102 & p104)

Una Flynn, Westmeath: loves to walk the Royal Canal (p48)

Marie McGuirk

Marie McGuirk trained as a Domestic Science teacher in Garnerville College, now part of Ulster University, where she also completed a final year specialising in catering subjects. After a stint in a South African Missions School, Marie taught in Newry Catering College for two years. She joined An Grianán in 1978, where she coordinates and teaches courses in cooking and nutrition.

Marie has been a familiar face on Irish television for several generations, appearing as a regular contributor to *Live at Three* for many years. More recently she was one of the 4 *Live* judges for their Domestic Goddess competition, and was one of the ICA mentors on ICA *Bootcamp*.

Her recipes appear fortnightly in *Woman's Way* magazine and monthly in *The Sacred Heart Messenger*, and she has produced two cookery books, *Foodalicious* and *Foodalicious Second Helpings*.

Edward Hayden

Well-known freelance chef from TV3's *Ireland* AM and author of *Food To Love* and *Edward Entertains*, Edward has a wealth of culinary experience from his training in Waterford IT and Cork IT and recently completed a Master's Degree in Learning & Teaching.

As well as lecturing full-time in Waterford IT in Culinary Arts and Hospitality Studies, Edward presents cookery demonstrations and classes in a variety of cookery schools and venues nationwide. He recently undertook a national cookery roadshow with the Irish Countrywomen's Association.

Edward's recipes regularly feature in a variety of local and national publications. For more information and recipes and to purchase *Edward Entertains* and *Food To Love*, see www.edwardentertains.com.

An Grianán adult education centre

As every ICA woman knows, An Grianán means 'sunny place' in Irish. This unique centre of life-long learning is the jewel in our crown and brings ICA women from all over the country to Termonfeckin, Co Louth.

Originally known as Newtown House, the property was built by the McClintock family in the 18th Century and sold to Mrs Helen Lentaigne in 1922. The first President of Termonfeckin ICA, Mrs Lentaigne allowed the newly constituted Irish Countrywomen's Association (founded as United Irishwomen in 1910) to use Newtown House as a venue for the ICA Summer School in the 1930s. Having changed hands several times in the 1940s, it was finally bought by the WK Kellogg Foundation in 1954 for £11,250 and entrusted to the Irish Countrywomen's Association for 'the health, education and welfare of the people of Ireland'.

Today, An Grianán operates as a unique residential centre, combining four-star accommodation with courses and classes in art, crafts, cookery, personal development and self-care for men, women and children as individuals or in groups. Set within 75 acres of wooded land, ornamental gardens and boasting a variety of amenities (including the Gatehouse Tea Rooms, Sanctuary Beauty Salon, Garden Centre and Muriel Gahan ICA Museum) An Grianán has been a haven of learning for the last 60-odd years.

Historic Members of the ICA

A short history of some of the ground-breaking
work of ICA women

Throughout the history of the ICA many important projects were undertaken by some courageous and forward-thinking women. The following is a highlight of just a few of those, but of course they could not have done it without the support and comradeship of grassroots ICA members nationwide.

Dr Muriel Gahan [1897–1995] is best known for her role in establishing The Country Shop on St Stephen's Green in 1930. Travelling the country in search of a weaver who could demonstrate the craft at a show in the Royal Dublin Society, Muriel had been struck by the very many women trying to make some money by selling crafts produced at home. She was inspired to set up The Country Shop in order to give these small producers a marketplace in Dublin. Over time, Country Markets became established throughout Ireland and these are still an important part of Irish life today. Muriel's work is celebrated by the ICA in the Muriel Gahan Museum in An Grianán. She is also well remembered by the ICA, which has adopted her motto for life, 'Deeds Not Words'. Muriel was awarded an honorary doctorate by Trinity College Dublin in recognition of all her work.

Eleanora Gibbon [1876–1953] set up the 'Casa Dei Bambini' or Children's House in the Convent of Mercy Waterford together with Sister Gertrude Allman after both women attended a training course in London run by Maria Montessori. Eleanora encouraged the establishment of Montessori schools throughout Waterford and Ireland, and went on to teach in many schools in Waterford and to write the book *Ireland, Freedom and the Child*, published in 1943. She is commemorated by the ICA in their annual competitions for the Eleanora Gibbon Shield for Singing in Irish and the Eleanora Gibbon Cup for Drama. Eleanora's family kindly donated the Shield and Cup to help keep her love of music and drama alive in the ICA.

Nora Herlihy [1911–1988] was a teacher and member of Ballydesmond Guild, Dublin Federation. She was a founding member of the Dublin Central Co-operative Society Ltd (DCCS), which led to the establishment of the Co-operative movement in Ireland in 1954. Nora held a very instrumental role as chair of the original DCCS meetings and together with Muriel Gahan and others went on to fund the Credit Union Movement with funds from the United Irishwomen. Nora remained very much involved with the Credit Union and the ICA for the rest of her life.

Olivia Hughes [1908–1989] was a woman of vision and a pioneer in many fields who went on to become National President of the ICA from 1955–58. In 1926 she reformed the Fethard Branch of the United Irishwomen, as the ICA was then known. Under her direction the Branch established milk depots and opened a canteen at fairs serving tea, coffee, bovril and sandwiches, a service run voluntarily on a rota basis. This continued until the marts replaced fairs in the 1950s. She became a great promoter of crafts and was instrumental, amongst other, in organising the first ICA summer school, held in Sliabh na mBán, Co Tipperary in 1929. She was also involved in the setting up of both the National Council for the Blind and the Horticultural College at An Grianán.

Acknowledgements

Liz Wall, National President of the ICA, would like to thank the following people for all of their help with putting together this wonderful ICA recipe book:

Marie McGuirk, Resident Chef in An Grianán, for that long, hot week in May when she cooked and tested every single recipe in this book.

Edward Hayden for all his wonderful ICA cookery events and his contributions to this book.

John O'Callaghan, CEO of the ICA, for his support to all recipe contributors and staff members.

Joanne Dunne in ICA Central Office for all her work on collecting recipe waivers.

Rebecca Ryan in ICA Central Office for her work on the copy.

Ann Flanagan, Manager of An Grianán, for her unending help and support to all of us.

Aoife Carrigy for her determined professionalism in ensuring our cookbook is one we are all proud of.

Orla Neligan for styling the dishes so sensitively and **Joanne Murphy** for photographing them so beautifully.

Finally to all the great people at Gill & Macmillan for their hard work in making our cookbook a reality.

List of Photographs

All photographs were taken on site at An Grianán in Termonfeckin, Co Louth. The following captions relate to the non-food photographs through the book, including many items on display at the Muriel Gahan ICA Museum, located in the coffeeshop at An Grianán.

Page V: Yellow roses in full bloom outside the entrance of An Grianán adult education centre. Originally known as Newtown House, the 18th-century property was entrusted to the ICA in 1954.

Page VI: One of the earliest Jackson Electric Cooker models with four solid rings, on display in the Muriel Gahan ICA Museum at An Grianán together with three-legged cast iron pot, casserole, pressure cooker and toasting fork. Rural electrification was introduced in the 1950s and transformed the lives of Irish women.

Page XII: An original 1950s Electrolux fridge, donated from Fethard, South Tipperary, topped with table churn and butter pats for making country butter and an earthenware water jug. All these items are on display in the Muriel Gahan ICA Museum at An Grianán.

Page XVIII: Silverware would traditionally have been reserved for special occasions in most households.

Page 26: On display in An Grianán's Museum, traditional Leitrim chairs surround a wooden kitchen table. This is set with a wooden bread-making pan and right-angled ladle used for

dough-cutting, butter-making and other purposes. On the windowsill sit a wooden mixing bowl, Victorian metal jelly mould and earthenware water jug.

Page 28: Carving platter and implements for the traditional Sunday roast.

Page 84: An Grianán's avenue sweeps 500 metres from the gates just outside Termonfeckin past self-catering accommodation units, coffeeshop and garden centre to the 18th-century house.

Page 98: An Grianán is surrounded by 75 acres of rapeseed fields, woodlands and ornamental gardens.

Page 189: An old-fashioned iron dating from pre-electrification. The Muriel Gahan ICA Museum are in continual receipt of these historic household items kindly donated by members and their families.

Page 190: Yellow roses in full bloom outside the entrance of An Grianán adult education centre. Originally known as Newtown House, the 18th-century property was entrusted to the ICA in 1954.